LETTERS AND LESSONS
OF TEDDY ROOSEVELT
FOR HIS SONS

LETTERS AND LESSONS OF TEDDY ROOSEVELT FOR HIS SONS

Edited and Compiled by
Douglas W. Phillips

THE VISION FORUM, INC.
SAN ANTONIO, TEXAS

The Vision Forum, Inc.
4719 Blanco Rd.
San Antonio, Texas 78212
1-800-440-0022
www.visionforum.com

"Where there is no vision the people perish."

ISBN: 1-929241-32-1

Typography and Cover Design by Joshua R. Goforth

Printed in the United States of America

Dedication

For my beloved friend and brother,
Richard "Little Bear" Wheeler,
a man who has taught an entire generation of boys
to live clean and virtuous lives.
Teddy would have been proud.

Contents

Teddy, the Father of Boys

The future of a country can in part be measured by its ability to produce heroic young men of faith and virtue. It was not until the horror of September 11, 2001, that Americans, for the first time in half a century, began to once again whisper about the importance of training boys to be protectors and defenders of women and children. Images of fire fighting men dashing into burning buildings and reports of young fathers rushing hijackers on a doomed airline flight have reminded us that there is great nobility in masculinity. Even more significantly, they have raised the possibility that the old Christian idea that boys should be trained to embrace chivalric concepts of leadership, self-sacrifice, and virtue must once again be revived if we as a people will survive the many challenges of the next century.

The purpose of this book is to introduce you to a man who understood the relationship between boyhood, masculinity, leadership, strenuous living, and the future success of the American people. Here is a man who rejoiced in fatherhood, who saw it as his mission to raise sturdy boys, and who just happened to be one of the greatest public figures in our nation's illustrious history.

Over the course of his life, Theodore Roosevelt delivered an untold number of speeches and produced more original books than any other president in United States history, but when asked of the work he was most proud to have published, he declared that it was his letters to his children.

David McCullough, the famed biographer of John Adams, once observed that heroes are not gods. If they were gods, we would expect them to behave perfectly. What makes them great is that they were imperfect men who acted extraordinarily when it mattered.

And so it is with Teddy, the father of four boys. Roosevelt was not a perfect father. Some might argue that those imperfections would later manifest themselves in the life of at least one of his sons, Kermit, who died tragically, never ultimately reconciling himself to his role as the progeny of a truly iconic father. And yet, even Kermit, the one Roosevelt son who could be described as "troubled," not only adored his father, but intellectually embraced his father's life ethic. On one occasion during a jungle expedition accident, Kermit refused to listen to his injured father's request to leave him behind to die and demonstrated tremendous bravery and self-sacrifice, ultimately saving his father's life.

Where Teddy was strong as a father, he was very strong. He passionately loved his sons. What is more, he let them know that he loved them...constantly. He spoke to them with both manly resolve and fatherly tenderness. He longed not only to be their leader, but their playmate and their friend. He regularly set aside his presidential duties to stop and read them the Bible, and he engaged them in the kinds of glorious discussions and debates that fathers should have with their maturing sons to help them hone their critical thinking skills.

At times he found himself divided between the obligations of running a country and raising children. But more often than not, Roosevelt demonstrated that being a father was more important to him than being president. And this is what makes him great. One observation to be drawn from his letters is that Roosevelt was quick to scrap his presidential responsibilities and focus on what lesser men would consider the trivial and unimportant duties of fatherhood...finding lizards with his sons, scrambling over rocks with them, or rejoicing in the smallest of their youthful victories and conquests.

Roosevelt was always thinking of his sons. He often brought them with him on his fantastic adventures around the world and wrote to them assiduously when he was separated from them. He was forever in search of interesting trinkets for his boys which would allow them to be part of their father's experiences. One observer noted that in the midst of heavy shelling during the battle for San Juan Hill, Roosevelt remained standing (seemingly impervious to the shelling all around him), notwithstanding the fact that people were falling to his right and left. The only time he ducked out of the range of bullets and shell fire was when it occurred to him to collect used cartridges for his sons as souvenirs.

As to the defense of America, Roosevelt instructed his boys that it was among their highest duties and privileges to defend their national boundaries and advance the cause of freedom. Edward J. Renehan writes of the boys that, "each came of age sharing Roosevelt's Kiplingesque view of the battlefield as a place of honor, fulfillment, and robust democracy." Yes, the man who taught America about "the strenuous life" practiced what he preached and taught his sons to do so as well.

The book in your hands is divided into three parts, each designed to offer a message from the past to the fathers and sons of the twenty-first century. The first part includes a selection of letters categorized by son and listed in chronological order. In the second part of the book, I have included Teddy's autobiographical accounts of his own childhood, youth and early manhood, including his romantic episode as a western cowboy. Each account offers rich insights into the development of the person many believed to be the quintessential example of bold manhood. The third and final part of the book is a collection of essays and speeches written by T.R., each of which offer sage counsel on the meaning of character and manhood.

For some years now it has been my privilege to walk down to the old Menger hotel (just yards from the Alamo) where Teddy recruited his Rough Riders. During those walks and times of reflection, I have reached the following conclusion concerning the true source of Teddy's greatness: Teddy Roosevelt was not great because of his politics, and he was not great because of his presidency. Roosevelt was great because he was an anti-cynic. He believed that right was right and that wrong was wrong, and that men can know the difference. He was great because he personified manhood during a transitional time in American history when the old Christian ideals of family and patriarchy first began to give sway to the egalitarian philosophies of modernity. Roosevelt was the last American leader to boldly proclaim over and over again that men were to be defenders of women. He was the last President to openly rejoice in fatherhood and to urge others to do the same. And, perhaps better than any other public figure in American history, Roosevelt was able to communicate a contagious zest for life.

With this in mind, I humbly submit to the reader this collection of letters, autobiographical accounts, and essays from a man who, first and foremost, wanted to be remembered as a father.

Douglas W. Phillips, Esq.
Publisher
San Antonio, Texas

PART I:

FATHER
AND SONS

THE LETTERS OF TEDDY TO HIS CHILDREN

By Joseph Bucklin Bishop (1847-1928)

The following commentary was written in 1919 by Teddy Roosevelt's friend and the editor of Theodore Roosevelt's Letter's To His Children. *Many of the letters originally published by Mr. Bishop are included in this volume. We have organized them differently, and offered fresh editorial comments.*—D.W.P.

Most of the letters in this volume were written by Theodore Roosevelt to his children during a period of more than twenty years. A few others are included that he wrote to friends or relatives about the children. He began to write to them in their early childhood, and continued to do so regularly till they reached maturity. Whenever he was separated from them, in the Spanish War, or on a hunting trip, or because they were at school, he sent them these messages of constant thought and love, for they were never for a moment out of his mind and heart. Long before they were able to read he sent them what they called "picture letters," with crude drawings of his own in illustration of the written text, drawings precisely adapted to the childish imagination and intelligence. That the little recipients cherished these delightful missives is shown by the tender care with which they preserved them from destruction. They are in good condition after many years of loving usage. A few of them are reproduced in these pages—written at different periods as each new child appeared in the household.

These early letters are marked by the same quality that distinguishes all his letters to his children. From the youngest to the eldest, he wrote to them always as his equals. As they advanced in life the mental level of intercourse was raised as they grew in intelligence and knowledge, but it was always as equals that he addressed them. He was always their playmate and boon companion, whether they were toddling infants taking their first faltering steps, or growing schoolboys, or youths standing at the threshold of life. Their games were his games, their joys those of his own heart. He was ready to romp with them in the old barn at Sagamore Hill, play "tickley" at bedtime, join in their pillow fights, or play hide-and-seek with them, either at Sagamore Hill or in the White House. He was the same chosen and joyous companion always and everywhere. Occasionally he was disturbed for a moment about possible injury to his Presidential dignity. Describing a romp in the old barn at Sagamore Hill in the summer of 1903, he said in one of his letters that under the insistence of the children he had joined in it because: "I had not the heart to refuse, but really it seems, to put it mildly, rather odd for a stout, elderly President to be bouncing over hayricks in a wild effort to get to goal before an active midget of a competitor, aged nine years. However, it was really great fun."

It was because he at heart regarded it as "great fun" and was in complete accord with the children that they delighted in him as a playmate. In the same spirit, in January, 1905, he took a squad of nine boys, including three of his own, on what they called a "scramble" through Rock Creek Park, in Washington, which meant traversing the most difficult places in it. The boys had permission to make the trip alone, but they insisted upon his company. "I am really touched," he wrote afterward to the parents of two of the visiting boys, "at the way in which your children as well as my own treat me as a friend and playmate. It has its comic side. They were all bent upon having me take them; they obviously felt that my presence was needed to give zest to the entertainment. I do not think that one of them saw anything incongruous in the President's getting as bedaubed with mud as they got, or in my wiggling and clambering around jutting rocks, through cracks, and up what were really small cliff faces, just like the rest of them; and whenever any one of them beat me at any point, he felt and expressed simple and whole-hearted delight, exactly as if it had been a triumph over a rival of his own age."

When the time came that he was no longer the children's chosen playmate, he recognized the fact with a twinge of sadness. Writing in January, 1905, to his daughter Ethel, who was at Sagamore Hill at the time, he said of a party of boys that Quentin had at the White House: "They played hard, and it made me realize how old I had grown and how very busy I had been the last few years to find that they had grown so that I was not needed in the play. Do you recollect how all of us used to play hide and go seek in the White House, and have obstacle races down the hall when you brought in your friends?"

Deep and abiding love of children, of family and home, that was the dominating passion of his life. With that went love for friends and fellow men, and for all living things, birds, animals, trees, flowers, and nature in all its moods and aspects. But love of children and family and home was above all. The children always had an old-fashioned Christmas in the White House. In several letters in these pages, descriptions of these festivals will be found. In closing one of them the eternal child's heart in the man cries out: "I wonder whether there ever can come in life a thrill of greater exaltation and rapture than that which comes to one between the ages of say six and fourteen, when the library door is thrown open and you walk in to see all the gifts, like a materialized fairy land, arrayed on your special table?"

His love for the home he had built and in which his beloved children had been born, was not even dimmed by his life in the White House. "After all," he wrote to Ethel in June, 1906, "fond as I am of the White House and much though I have appreciated these years in it, there isn't any place in the world like home—like Sagamore Hill, where things are our own, with their own associations, and where it is real country."

Through all his letters runs his inexhaustible vein of delicious humor. All the quaint sayings of Quentin, that quaintest of small boys; all the antics of the household cats and dogs; all the comic aspects of the guinea-pigs and others of the large menagerie of pets that the children were always collecting; all the tricks and feats of the saddle-horses—these, together with every item of household news that would amuse and cheer and keep alive the love of home in the heart of the absent boys, was set forth in letters which in gayety of spirit and charm of manner have few equals in literature and no superiors. No matter how great the pressure of public duties, or how severe the strain that the trials and burdens of office placed upon the nerves and spirits of the President of a great nation, this devoted father and whole-hearted companion found time to send every week a long letter of this delightful character to each of his absent children.

As the boys advanced toward manhood the letters, still on the basis of equality, contain much wise suggestion and occasional admonition, the latter always administered in a loving spirit accompanied by apology for writing in a "preaching" vein. The playmate of childhood became the sympathetic and keenly interested companion in all athletic contests, in the reading of books and the consideration of authors, and in the discussion of politics and public affairs. Many of these letters, notably those on the relative merits of civil and military careers, and the proper proportions of sport and study, are valuable guides for youth in all ranks of life. The strong, vigorous, exalted character of the writer stands revealed in these as in all the other letters, as well as the cheerful soul of the man which remained throughout his life as pure and gentle as the soul of a child. (Only a short time before he died, he said to me, as we were going over the letters and planning this volume, which is arranged as he wished it to be.)

Letters to
Teddy, Jr.

Hunting the Cougar
Ranch, Colo., Jan. 14th, 1901.

Blessed Ted,

From the railroad we drove fifty miles to the little frontier town of Meeker. There we were met by the hunter Goff, a fine, quiet, hardy fellow, who knows his business thoroughly. Next morning we started on horseback, while our luggage went by wagon to Goff's ranch. We started soon after sunrise, and made our way, hunting as we went, across the high, exceedingly rugged hills, until sunset. We were hunting cougar and lynx or, as they are called out here, "lion" and "cat." The first cat we put up gave the dogs a two hours' chase, and got away among some high cliffs. In the afternoon we put up another, and had a very good hour's run, the dogs baying until the glens rang again to the echoes, as they worked hither and thither through the ravines. We walked our ponies up and down steep, rock-strewn, and tree-clad slopes, where it did not seem possible a horse could climb, and on the level places we got one or two smart gallops. At last the lynx went up a tree. Then I saw a really funny sight. Seven hounds had been doing the trailing, while a large brindled bloodhound and two half-breeds between collie and bull stayed behind Goff, running so close to his horse's heels that they continually bumped into them, which he accepted with philosophic composure. Then the dogs proceeded literally to climb the tree, which was a many-forked pinon; one of the half-breeds, named Tony, got up certainly sixteen feet, until the lynx, which looked like a huge and exceedingly malevolent pussy-cat, made vicious dabs at him. I shot the lynx low, so as not to hurt his skin.

Yesterday we were in the saddle for ten hours. The dogs ran one lynx down and killed it among the rocks after a vigorous scuffle. It was in a hole and only two of them could get at it.

This morning, soon after starting out, we struck the cold trail of a mountain lion. The hounds puzzled about for nearly two hours, going up and down the great gorges, until we sometimes absolutely lost even the sound of the baying. Then they struck the fresh trail, where the cougar had killed a deer over night. In half an hour a clamorous yelling told us they had overtaken the quarry; for we had been riding up the slopes and along the crests, wherever it was possible for the horses to get footing. As we plunged and scrambled down towards the noise, one of my companions, Phil Stewart, stopped us while he took a kodak of a rabbit which sat unconcernedly right beside our path. Soon we saw the lion in a treetop, with two of the dogs so high up among the branches that he was striking at them. He was more afraid of us than of the dogs, and as soon as he saw us he took a great flying leap and was off, the pack close behind. In a few hundred yards they had him up another tree. Here I could have shot him (Tony climbed almost up to him, and then fell twenty feet out of the tree), but waited for Stewart to get a photo; and he jumped again. This time, after a couple of hundred yards, the dogs caught him, and a great fight followed. They could have killed him by themselves, but he bit or clawed four of them, and for fear he might kill one I ran in and stabbed him behind the shoulder, thrusting the knife you loaned me right into his heart. I have always wished to kill a cougar as I did this one, with dogs and the knife.

ADVICE ON STUDIES
Oyster Bay, May 7th, 1901.

Blessed Ted,

It was the greatest fun seeing you, and I really had a satisfactory time with you, and came away feeling that you were doing well. I am entirely satisfied with your standing, both in your studies and in athletics. I want you to do well in your sports, and I want even more to have you do well with your books; but I do not expect you to stand first in either, if so to stand could cause you overwork and hurt your health. I always believe in going hard at everything, whether it is Latin or mathematics, boxing or football, but at the same time I want to keep the sense of proportion. It is never worth while to absolutely exhaust one's self or to take big chances unless for an adequate object. I want you to keep in training the faculties which would make you, if the need arose, able to put your last ounce of pluck and strength into a contest. But I do not want you to squander these qualities. To have you play football as well as you do, and make a good name in boxing and wrestling, and be cox of your second crew, and stand second or third in your class in the studies, is all right. I should be rather sorry to see you drop too near the middle of your class, because, as you cannot enter college until you are nineteen, and will therefore be a year later in entering life, I want you to be prepared in the best possible way, so as to make up for the delay. But I know that all you can do you will do to keep substantially the position in the class that you have so far kept, and I have entire trust in you, for you have always deserved it.

The weather has been lovely here. The cherry trees are in full bloom, the peach trees just opening, while the apples will not be out for ten days. The May flowers and bloodroot have gone, the anemonies and bellwort have come and the violets are coming. All the birds are here, pretty much, and the warblers troop through the woods.

To my delight, yesterday Kermit, when I tried him on Diamond, did excellently. He has evidently turned the corner in his riding, and was just as much at home as possible, although he was on my saddle with his feet thrust in the leathers above the stirrup. Poor mother has had a hard time with Yagenka, for she rubbed her back, and as she sadly needs exercise and I could not have a saddle put upon her, I took her out bareback yesterday. Her gaits are so easy that it is really more comfortable to ride her without a saddle than to ride Texas with one, and I gave her three miles sharp cantering and trotting.

Dewey Jr. is a very cunning white guinea pig. I wish you could see Kermit taking out Dewey Sr. and Bob Evans to spend the day on the grass. Archie is the sweetest little fellow imaginable. He is always thinking of you. He has now struck up a great friendship with Nicholas, rather to Mame's (the nurse's) regret, as Mame would like to keep him purely for Quentin. The last-named small boisterous person was in fearful disgrace this morning, having flung a block at his mother's head. It was done in sheer playfulness, but of course could not be passed over lightly, and after the enormity of the crime had been brought fully home to him, he fled with howls of anguish to me and lay in an abandon of yellow-headed grief in my arms. Ethel is earning money for the purchase of the Art Magazine by industriously hoeing up the weeds in the walk. Alice is going to ride Yagenka bareback this afternoon, while I try to teach Ethel on Diamond, after Kermit has had his ride.

Yesterday at dinner we were talking of how badly poor Mrs. Blank looked, and Kermit suddenly observed in an aside to Ethel, entirely unconscious that we were listening: "Oh, Effel, I'll tell you what Mrs. Blank looks like: Like Davis' hen dat died—you know, de one dat couldn't hop up on de perch." Naturally, this is purely a private anecdote.

WRESTLE BEFORE DINNER, NOT BED
Oyster Bay, May 7, 1901.

Blessed Ted,

Recently I have gone in to play with Archie and Quentin after they have gone to bed, and they have grown to expect me, jumping up, very soft and warm in their tommies, expecting me to roll them over on the bed and tickle and "grabble" in them. However, it has proved rather too exciting, and an edict has gone forth that hereafter I must play bear with them before supper, and give up the play when they have gone to bed. To-day was Archie's birthday, and Quentin resented Archie's having presents while he (Quentin) had none. With the appalling frankness of three years old, he remarked with great sincerity that "it made him miserable," and when taken to task for his lack of altruistic spirit he expressed an obviously perfunctory repentance and said: "Well, boys must lend boys things, at any rate!"

THE SAN FRANSICSO EXPOSITION
Oyster Bay, May 31st, 1901.

Blessed Ted,

I enclose some Filipino Revolutionary postage stamps. Maybe some of the boys would like them.

Have you made up your mind whether you would like to try shooting the third week in August or the last week in July, or would you rather wait until you come back when I can find out something more definite from Mr. Post?

We very much wished for you while we were at the (San Francisco) Exposition. By night it was especially beautiful. Alice and I also wished that you could have been with us when we were out riding at Geneseo. Major Wadsworth put me on a splendid big horse called Triton, and sister on a thoroughbred mare. They would jump anything. It was sister's first experience, but she did splendidly and rode at any fence at which I would first put Triton. I did not try anything very high, but still some of the posts and rails were about four feet high, and it was enough to test sister's seat. Of course, all we had to do was to stick on as the horses jumped perfectly and enjoyed it quite as much as we did. The first four or five fences that I went over I should be ashamed to say how far I bounced out of the saddle, but after a while I began to get into my seat again. It has been a good many years since I have jumped a fence.

Mother stopped off at Albany while sister went on to Boston, and I came on here alone Tuesday afternoon. St. Gaudens, the sculptor, and Dunne (Mr. Dooley) were on the train and took lunch with us. It was great fun meeting them and I liked them both. Kermit met me in high feather, although I did not reach the house until ten o'clock, and he sat by me and we exchanged anecdotes while I took my supper. Ethel had put an alarm clock under her head so as to be sure and wake up, but although it went off she continued to slumber profoundly, as did Quentin. Archie waked up sufficiently to tell me that he had found another turtle just as small as the already existing treasure of the same kind. This morning Quentin and Black Jack have neither of them been willing to leave me for any length of time. Black Jack simply lies curled up in a chair, but as Quentin is most conversational, he has added an element of harassing difficulty to my effort to answer my accumulated correspondence.

Archie announced that he had seen "the Baltimore orioles catching fish!" This seemed to warrant investigation; but it turned out he meant barn swallows skimming the water.

The President not only sent "picture letters" to his own children, but an especial one to Miss Sarah Schuyler Butler, daughter of Dr. Nicholas Murray Butler, President of Columbia University, who had written to him a little note of congratulation on his first birthday in the White House.

Passing On Dad's Rifle
Oyster Bay, Aug. 25, 1903.

Dear Ted:

We have thought of you a good deal, of course. I am glad you have my rifle with you—you scamp, does it still have "those associations" which you alleged as the reason why you would value it so much when in the near future I became unable longer to use it? I do not have very much hope of your getting a great deal of sport on this trip, and anything you do get in the way of furred or feathered game and fishing I shall count as so much extra thrown in; but I feel the trip will teach you a lot in the way of handling yourself in a wild country, as well as of managing horses and camp outfits—of dealing with frontiersmen, etc. It will therefore fit you to go on a regular camping trip next time.

I have sternly refused to allow mother to ride Wyoming, on the ground that I would not have her make a martyr of herself in the shape of riding a horse with a single-foot gait, which she so openly detests. Accordingly, I have had some long and delightful rides with her, she on Yagenka and I on Bleistein, while Ethel and Kermit have begun to ride Wyoming. Kermit was with us this morning and got along beautifully till we galloped, whereupon Wyoming made up his mind that it was a race, and Kermit, for a moment or two, found him a handful.

On Sunday, after we came back from church and bathed, I rowed mother out to the end of Lloyds Neck, near your favorite camping ground. There we took lunch and spent a couple of hours with our books, reading a little and looking out over the beautiful Sound and at the headlands and white beaches of the coast. We rowed back through a strange, shimmering sunset.

I have played a little tennis since you left. Winty Chandler beat me two sets, but I beat him one. Alex Russell beat me a long deuce set, 10 to 8. To-day the smaller children held their championship. Nick won a long deuce set from Archie, and to my surprise Oliver and Ethel beat Kermit and Philip in two straight sets. I officiated as umpire and furnished the prizes, which were penknives.

THE PLACE OF ATHLETICS
White House, Oct. 4, 1903.

Dear Ted:

In spite of the "Hurry! Hurry!" on the outside of your envelope, I did not like to act until I had consulted Mother and thought the matter over; and to be frank with you, old fellow, I am by no means sure that I am doing right now. If it were not that I feel you will be so bitterly disappointed, I would strongly advocate your acquiescing in the decision to leave you off the second squad this year. I am proud of your pluck, and I greatly admire football—though it was not a game I was ever able to play myself, my qualities resembling Kermit's rather than yours. But the very things that make it a good game make it a rough game, and there is always the chance of your being laid up. Now, I should not in the least object to your being laid up for a season if you were striving for something worth while, to get on the Groton school team, for instance, or on your class team when you entered Harvard—for of course I don't think you will have the weight to entitle you to try for the varsity. But I am by no means sure that it is worth your while to run the risk of being laid up for the sake of playing in the second squad when you are a fourth former, instead of when you are a fifth former. I do not know that the risk is balanced by the reward. However, I have told the Rector that as you feel so strongly about it, I think that the chance of your damaging yourself in body is outweighed by the possibility of bitterness of spirit if you could not play. Understand me, I should think mighty little of you if you permitted chagrin to make you bitter on some point where it was evidently right for you to suffer the chagrin. But in this case I am uncertain, and I shall give you the benefit of the doubt. If, however, the coaches at any time come to the conclusion that you ought not to be in the second squad, why you must come off without grumbling.

I am delighted to have you play football. I believe in rough, manly sports. But I do not believe in them if they degenerate into the sole end of any one's existence. I don't want you to sacrifice standing well in your studies to any over-athleticism; and I need not tell you that character counts for a great deal more than either intellect or body in winning success in life. Athletic proficiency is a mighty good servant, and like so many other good servants, a mighty bad master. Did you ever read Pliny's letter to Trajan, in which he speaks of its being advisable to keep the Greeks absorbed in athletics, because it distracted their minds from all serious pursuits, including soldiering, and prevented their ever being dangerous to the Romans? I have not a doubt that the British officers in the Boer War had their efficiency partly reduced because they had sacrificed their legitimate duties to an inordinate and ridiculous love of sports. A man must develop his physical prowess up to a certain point; but after he has reached that point there are other things that count more. In my regiment nine-tenths of the men were better horsemen than I was, and probably two-thirds of them better shots than I was, while on the average they were certainly hardier and more enduring. Yet after I had had them a very short while they all knew, and I knew too, that nobody else could command them as I could. I am glad you should play football; I am glad that you should box; I am glad that you should ride and shoot and walk and row as well as you do. I should be very sorry if you did not do these things. But don't ever get into the frame of mind which regards these things as constituting the end to which all your energies must be devoted, or even the major portion of your energies.

Yes, I am going to speak at Groton on prize day. I felt that while I was President, and while you and Kermit were at Groton I wanted to come up there and see you, and the Rector wished me to speak, and so I am very glad to accept.

By the way, I am working hard to get Renown accustomed to automobiles. He is such a handful now when he meets them that I seriously mind encountering them when Mother is along. Of course I do not care if I am alone, or with another man, but I am uneasy all the time when I am out with Mother. Yesterday I tried Bleistein over the hurdles at Chevy Chase. The first one was new, high and stiff, and the old rascal never rose six inches, going slap through it. I took him at it again and he went over all right.

I am very busy now, facing the usual endless worry and discouragement, and trying to keep steadily in mind that I must not only be as resolute as Abraham Lincoln in seeking to achieve decent ends, but as patient, as uncomplaining, and as even-tempered in dealing, not only with knaves, but with the well-meaning foolish people, educated and uneducated, who by their unwisdom give the knaves their chance.

ASSESSING RISK OF INJURY
White House, Oct. 11, 1903.

Dear Ted:

I have received letters from the Rector, from Mr. Woods, and from Mr. Billings. They all say that you should play on the third squad, and Mr. Woods says you are now satisfied to do so. This was my first, and as I am convinced, my real judgment in the case. If you get mashed up now in a serious way it may prevent your playing later. As I think I wrote you, I do not in the least object to your getting smashed if it is for an object that is worth while, such as playing on the Groton team or playing on your class team when you get to Harvard. But I think it a little silly to run any imminent risk of a serious smash simply to play on the second squad instead of the third.

I am judging for you as I would for myself. When I was young and rode across country I was light and tough, and if I did, as actually happened, break an arm or a rib no damage ensued and no scandal was caused. Now I am stiff and heavy, and any accident to me would cause immense talk, and I do not take the chance; simply because it is not worth while. On the other hand, if I should now go to war and have a brigade as I had my regiment before Santiago, I should take any chance that was necessary; because it would be worth while. In other words, I want to make the risk to a certain accident commensurate with the object gained.

DAD ADMITS HIS BODY IS FAILING
White House, Oct. 24, 1903.

Dear Ted:

I am really greatly pleased at your standing so high in your form, and I am sure that this year it is better for you to be playing where you are in football. I suppose next year you will go back to your position of end, as you would hardly be heavy enough for playing back, or to play behind the centre, against teams with big fellows. I repeat that your standing in the class gave me real pleasure. I have sympathized so much with your delight in physical prowess and have been so glad at the success you have had, that sometimes I have been afraid I have failed to emphasize sufficiently the fact that of course one must not subordinate study and work to the cultivation of such prowess. By the way, I am sorry to say that I am falling behind physically. The last two or three years I have had a tendency to rheumatism, or gout, or something of the kind, which makes me very stiff.

Renown is behaving better about automobiles and the like. I think the difference is largely in the way I handle him. He is a very good-natured and gentle horse, but timid and not over-wise, and when in a panic his great strength makes him well-nigh uncontrollable. Accordingly, he is a bad horse to try to force by anything. If possible, it is much better to give him a little time, and bring him up as gently as may be to the object of terror. When he behaves well I lean forward and give him a lump of sugar, and now the old boy eagerly puts around his head when I stretch out my hand. Bleistein I have ridden very little, because I think one of his forelegs is shaky, and I want to spare him all I can. Mother and I have had the most lovely rides imaginable.

HARVARD VS. YALE
White House, Nov. 4, 1903.

Dear Ted:

Three cheers for Groton! It was first-class.

On election day I saw the house, and it was all so lovely that I felt fairly homesick to be back in it. The Japanese maples were still in full leaf and were turning the most beautiful shades of scarlet imaginable. The old barn, I am sorry to say, seems to be giving away at one end.

Renown now behaves very well about automobiles, and indeed about everything. He is, however, a little touched in the wind. Bleistein, in spite of being a little shaky in one foreleg, is in splendid spirits and eager for any amount of go. When you get on here for the Christmas holidays you will have to try them both, for if there is any fox hunting I am by no means sure you will find it better to take Bleistein than Renown. Sister is very handsome and good, having had a delightful time.

That was a funny trick which the Indians played against Harvard. Harvard did well to play such a successful uphill game in the latter part of the second half as to enable them to win out; but I do not see how she stands a chance of success against Yale this year.

Passing on History Books
White House, November 28, 1903.

Dear Ted:

If I were you I should certainly get the best ankle support possible. You do not want to find next fall that Webb beats you for end because your ankle gives out and his does not. If I were in your place, if it were necessary, I should put the ankle in plaster for the next three weeks, or for as long as the doctor thinks it needful, rather than run any risk of this. At any rate, I would consult him and wear whatever he thinks is the right.

If I give it to you you must be very careful of it, because he sent it to me himself.

I wonder if you are old enough yet to care for a good history of the American Revolution. If so, I think I shall give you mine by Sir George Trevelyan; although it is by an Englishman, I really think it on the whole the best account I have.

P. S.-The Bond parrot for mother has turned up; it is a most meritorious parrot, very friendly, and quite a remarkable talker.

WASHINGTON'S AT VALLEY FORGE
White House, June 21, 1904.

Dear Ted:

Mother and I had a most lovely ride the other day, way up beyond Sligo Creek to what is called North-west Branch, at Burnt Mills, where is a beautiful gorge, deep and narrow, with great boulders and even cliffs. Excepting Great Falls it is the most beautiful place around here. Mother scrambled among the cliffs in her riding habit, very pretty and most interesting. The roads were good and some of the scenery really beautiful. We were gone four hours, half an hour being occupied with the scrambling in the gorge.

Saturday we went to the wedding of Teddy Douglas and Helen. It was a beautiful wedding in every way and I am very fond of both of them. Sunday we spent at Attorney-General Knox's at Valley Forge, and most unexpectedly I had to deliver a little address at the church in the afternoon, as they are trying to build a memorial to Washington. Think of the fact that in Washington's army that winter among the junior officers were Alexander Hamilton, Monroe, and Marshall— a future President of the United States, the future Chief Justice who was to do such wonderful work for our Government, and the man of most brilliant mind- Hamilton—whom we have ever developed in this country.

How To Handle College Critics
White House, October 2, 1905.

Consider the challenge of being the President's son and attending Harvard. Teddy, Jr., was dogged by reporters and subjected to some very unfortunate and untruthful published accounts of his doing. In true Rooseveltian fashion, his father sent him letters of encouragement, in which he shared his indignation for what was being done, and he offered solace to his first born son.—D.W.P.

Blessed Old Ted:

The thing to do is to go on just as you have evidently been doing, attract as little attention as possible, do not make a fuss about the newspaper men, camera creatures, and idiots generally, letting it be seen that you do not like them and avoid them, but not letting them betray you into any excessive irritation. I believe they will soon drop you, and it is just an unpleasant thing that you will have to live down. Ted, I have had an enormous number of unpleasant things that I have had to live down in my life at different times and you have begun to have them now. I saw that you were not out on the football field on Saturday and was rather glad of it, as evidently those infernal idiots were eagerly waiting for you, but whenever you do go you will have to make up your mind that they will make it exceedingly unpleasant for you for once or twice, and you will just have to bear it; for you can never in the world afford to let them drive you away from anything you intend to do, whether it is football or anything else, and by going about your own business quietly and pleasantly, doing just what you would do if they were not there, generally they will get tired of it, and the boys themselves will see that it is not your fault, and will feel, if anything, rather a sympathy for you. Meanwhile I want you to know that we are all thinking of you and sympathizing with you the whole time; and it is a great comfort to me to have such confidence in you and to know that though these creatures can cause you a little trouble and make you feel a little downcast, they can not drive you one way or the other, or make you alter the course you have set out for yourself.

We were all of us, I am almost ashamed to say, rather blue at getting back in the White House, simply because we missed Sagamore Hill so much. But it is very beautiful and we feel very ungrateful at having even a passing fit of blueness, and we are enjoying it to the full now. I have just seen Archie dragging some fifty foot of hose pipe across the tennis court to play in the sand-box. I have been playing tennis with Mr. Pinchot, who beat me three sets to one, the only deuce-set being the one I won.

This is just an occasion to show the stuff there is in you. Do not let these newspaper creatures and kindred idiots drive you one hair's breadth from the line you had marked out in football or anything else. Avoid any fuss, if possible.

LEARN TO IGNORE THE CRITICS
White House, October 11, 1905.

Dear Ted:

I was delighted to find from your last letters that you are evidently having a pretty good time in spite of the newspaper and kodak creatures. I guess that nuisance is now pretty well abated. Every now and then they will do something horrid; but I think you can safely, from now on, ignore them entirely.

I shall be interested to hear how you get on, first of all with your studies, in which you seem to have started well, and next with football. I expected that you would find it hard to compete with the other candidates for the position of end, as they are mostly heavier than you; especially since you went off in weight owing to the excitement of your last weeks of holiday in the summer. Of course the fact that you are comparatively light tells against you and gives you a good deal to overcome; and undoubtedly it was from this standpoint not a good thing that you were unable to lead a quieter life toward the end of your stay at Oyster Bay.

So it is about the polo club. In my day we looked with suspicion upon all freshman societies, and the men who tried to get them up or were prominent in them rarely amounted to much in the class afterwards; and it has happened that I have heard rather unfavorably of the polo club. But it may be mere accident that I have thus heard unfavorably about it, and in thirty years the attitude of the best fellows in college to such a thing as a freshman club may have changed so absolutely that my experience can be of no value. Exercise your own best judgment and form some idea of what the really best fellows in the class think on the subject. Do not make the mistake of thinking that the men who are merely undeveloped are really the best fellows, no matter how pleasant and agreeable they are or how popular. Popularity is a good thing, but it is not something for which to sacrifice studies or athletics or good standing in any way; and sometimes to seek it overmuch is to lose it. I do not mean this as applying to you, but as applying to certain men who still have a great vogue at first in the class, and of whom you will naturally tend to think pretty well.

In all these things I can only advise you in a very general way. You are on the ground. You know the men and the general college sentiment. You have gone in with the serious purpose of doing decently and honorably; of standing well in your studies; of showing that in athletics you mean business up to the extent of your capacity, and of getting the respect and liking of your classmates so far as they can be legitimately obtained. As to the exact methods of carrying out these objects, I must trust to you.

ON DICKENS, THACKERY, AND BUNYAN
White House, May 20, 1906.

Dear Ted:

Mother read us your note and I was interested in the discussion between you and _____ over Dickens. Dickens' characters are really to a great extent personified attributes rather than individuals. In consequence, while there are not nearly as many who are actually like people one meets, as for instance in Thackeray, there are a great many more who possess characteristics which we encounter continually, though rarely as strongly developed as in the fictional originals. So Dickens' characters last almost as Bunyan's do. For instance, Jefferson Brick and Elijah Pogram and Hannibal Chollop are all real personifications of certain bad tendencies in American life, and I am continually thinking of or alluding to some newspaper editor or Senator or homicidal rowdy by one of these three names. I never met any one exactly like Uriah Heep, but now and then we see individuals show traits which make it easy to describe them, with reference to those traits, as Uriah Heep. It is just the same with Micawber. Mrs. Nickleby is not quite a real person, but she typifies, in accentuated form, traits which a great many real persons possess, and I am continually thinking of her when I meet them. There are half a dozen books of Dickens which have, I think, furnished more characters which are the constant companions of the ordinary educated man around us, than is true of any other half-dozen volumes published within the same period.

PRIDE IN AMERICA
On Board U. S. S. Louisiana, Nov. 14., 1906.

Dear Ted:

I am very glad to have taken this trip, although as usual I am bored by the sea. Everything has been smooth as possible, and it has been lovely having Mother along. It gives me great pride in America to be aboard this great battleship and to see not only the material perfection of the ship herself in engines, guns, and all arrangements, but the fine quality of the officers and crew. Have you ever read Smollett's novel, I think "Roderick Random" or "Humphrey Clinker," in which the hero goes to sea? It gives me an awful idea of what a floating hell of filth, disease, tyranny, and cruelty a war-ship was in those days. Now every arrangement is as clean and healthful as possible. The men can bathe and do bathe as often as cleanliness requires. Their fare is excellent and they are as self-respecting a set as can be imagined. I am no great believer in the superiority of times past; and I have no question that the officers and men of our Navy now are in point of fighting capacity better than in the times of Drake and Nelson; and morally and in physical surroundings the advantage is infinitely in our favor.

It was delightful to have you two or three days at Washington. Blessed old fellow, you had a pretty hard time in college this fall; but it can't be helped, Ted; as one grows older the bitter and the sweet keep coming together. The only thing to do is to grin and bear it, to flinch as little as possible under the punishment, and to keep pegging steadily away until the luck turns.

News From Panama

U. S. S. Louisiana, At Sea, November 20, 1906.

Dear Ted:

This is the third day out from Panama. We have been steaming steadily in the teeth of the trade wind. It has blown pretty hard, and the ship has pitched a little, but not enough to make either Mother or me uncomfortable.

Panama was a great sight. In the first place it was strange and beautiful with its mass of luxuriant tropic jungle, with the treacherous tropic rivers trailing here and there through it; and it was lovely to see the orchids and brilliant butterflies and the strange birds and snakes and lizards, and finally the strange old Spanish towns and the queer thatch and bamboo huts of the ordinary natives. In the next place it is a tremendous sight to see the work on the canal going on. From the chief engineer and the chief sanitary officer down to the last arrived machinist or time-keeper, the five thousand Americans at work on the Isthmus seemed to me an exceptionally able, energetic lot, some of them grumbling, of course, but on the whole a mighty good lot of men. The West Indian negroes offer a greater problem, but they are doing pretty well also. I was astonished at the progress made. We spent the three days in working from dawn until long after darkness—dear Dr. Rixey being, of course, my faithful companion. Mother would see all she liked and then would go off on a little spree by herself, and she enjoyed it to the full.

On Bagging A Bear
En route to Washington, Oct. 22, 1907.

Dear Ted:

"Bad old father" is coming back after a successful trip. It was a success in every way, including the bear hunt; but in the case of the bear hunt we only just made it successful and no more, for it was not until the twelfth day of steady hunting that I got my bear. Then I shot it in the most approved hunter's style, going up on it in a canebrake as it made a walking bay before the dogs. I also killed a deer-more by luck than anything else, as it was a difficult shot.

LETTERS TO KERMIT

Focus On Your Latin
White House, Oct. 13, 1902.

Blessed Kermit:

I am delighted at all the accounts I receive of how you are doing at Groton. You seem to be enjoying yourself and are getting on well. I need not tell you to do your best to cultivate ability for concentrating your thought on whatever work you are given to do—you will need it in Latin especially. Who plays opposite you at end? Do you find you can get down well under the ball to tackle the full-back? How are you tackling?

Mother is going to present Gem to Uncle Will. She told him she did not think he was a good dog for the city; and therefore she gives him to Uncle Will to keep in the country. Uncle Will's emotion at such self-denying generosity almost overcame him. Gem is really a very nice small bow-wow, but Mother found that in this case possession was less attractive than pursuit. When she takes him out walking he carries her along as if she was a Roman chariot. She thinks that Uncle Will or Eda can anchor him. Yesterday she and Ethel held him and got burrs out of his hair. It was a lively time for all three.

THANKSGIVING IN THE WHITE HOUSE
White House, Nov. 28, 1902.

Darling Kermit:

Yesterday was Thanksgiving, and we all went out riding, looking as we started a good deal like the Cumberbach family. Archie on his beloved pony, and Ethel on Yagenka went off with Mr. Proctor to the hunt. Mother rode Jocko Root, Ted a first-class cavalry horse, I rode Renown, and with us went Senator Lodge, Uncle Douglas, Cousin John Elliott, Mr. Bob Fergie, and General Wood. We had a three hours' scamper which was really great fun

Yesterday I met Bozie for the first time since he came to Washington, and he almost wiggled himself into a fit, he was so overjoyed at renewing acquaintance. To see Jack and Tom Quartz play together is as amusing as it can be. We have never had a more cunning kitten than Tom Quartz. I have just had to descend with severity upon Quentin because he put the unfortunate Tom into the bathtub and then turned on the water. He didn't really mean harm.

Last evening, besides our own entire family party, all the Lodges, and their connections, came to dinner. We dined in the new State Dining-room and we drank the health of you and all the rest of both families that were absent. After dinner we cleared away the table and danced. Mother looked just as pretty as a picture and I had a lovely waltz with her. Mrs. Lodge and I danced the Virginia Reel.

Pets vs. The Speaker of the House
White House, Jan. 6, 1903.

Dear Kermit:

We felt very melancholy after you and Ted left and the house seemed empty and lonely. But it was the greatest possible comfort to feel that you both really have enjoyed school and are both doing well there.

Tom Quartz is certainly the cunningest kitten I have ever seen. He is always playing pranks on Jack and I get very nervous lest Jack should grow too irritated. The other evening they were both in the library—Jack sleeping before the fire—Tom Quartz scampering about, an exceedingly playful little wild creature—which is about what he is. He would race across the floor, then jump upon the curtain or play with the tassel. Suddenly he spied Jack and galloped up to him. Jack, looking exceedingly sullen and shame-faced, jumped out of the way and got upon the sofa, where Tom Quartz instantly jumped upon him again. Jack suddenly shifted to the other sofa, where Tom Quartz again went after him. Then Jack started for the door, while Tom made a rapid turn under the sofa and around the table, and just as Jack reached the door leaped on his hind-quarters. Jack bounded forward and away and the two went tandem out of the room—Jack not reappearing at all; and after about five minutes Tom Quartz stalked solemnly back.

Another evening the next Speaker of the House, Mr. Cannon, an exceedingly solemn, elderly gentleman with chin whiskers, who certainly does not look to be of playful nature, came to call upon me. He is a great friend of mine, and we sat talking over what our policies for the session should be until about eleven o'clock; and when he went away I accompanied him to the head of the stairs. He had gone about half-way down when Tom Quartz strolled by, his tail erect and very fluffy. He spied Mr. Cannon going down the stairs, jumped to the conclusion that he was a playmate escaping, and raced after him, suddenly grasping him by the leg the way he does Archie and Quentin when they play hide and seek with him; then loosening his hold he tore down-stairs ahead of Mr. Cannon, who eyed him with iron calm and not one particle of surprise.

Ethel has reluctantly gone back to boarding-school. It is just after lunch and Dulany is cutting my hair while I dictate this to Mr. Loeb. I left Mother lying on the sofa and reading aloud to Quentin, who as usual has hung himself over the back of the sofa in what I should personally regard as an exceedingly uncomfortable attitude to listen to literature. Archie we shall not see until this evening, when he will suddenly challenge me either to a race or a bear play, and if neither invitation is accepted will then propose that I tell a pig story or else read aloud from the Norse folk tales.

TREASURES FOR THE CHILDREN
Del Monte, Cal., May 10, 1903.

Blessed Kermit:

The last weeks' travel I have really enjoyed. Last Sunday and to-day (Sunday) and also on Wednesday at the Grand

Canyon I had long rides, and the country has been strange and beautiful. I have collected a variety of treasures, which I shall have to try to divide up equally among you children. One treasure, by the way, is a very small badger, which I named Josiah, and he is now called Josh for short. He is very cunning and I hold him in my arms and pet him. I hope he will grow up friendly—that is if the poor little fellow lives to grow up at all. Dulany is taking excellent care of him, and we feed him on milk and potatoes.

I have enjoyed meeting an old classmate of mine at Harvard. He was heavyweight boxing champion when I was in college.

I was much interested in your seeing the wild deer. That was quite remarkable. Today, by the way, as I rode along the beach I saw seals, cormorants, gulls and ducks, all astonishingly tame.

Boys Playing With Secret Service
Oyster Bay, Sept. 23, 1903.

Blessed Kermit:

The house seems very empty without you and Ted, although I cannot conscientiously say that it is quiet— Archie and Quentin attend to that. Archie, barefooted, bareheaded, and with his usual faded blue overalls, much torn and patched, has just returned from a morning with his beloved Nick. Quentin has passed the morning in sports and pastimes with the long-suffering secret service men.

Allan has been associating closely with mother and me. Yesterday Ethel went off riding with Lorraine. She rode Wyoming, who is really turning out a very good family horse. This evening I expect Grant La Farge and Owen Wister, who are coming to spend the night. Mother is as busy as possible putting up the house, and Ethel and I insist that she now eyes us both with a purely professional gaze, and secretly wishes she could wrap us up in a neatly pinned sheet with camphor balls inside. Good-bye, blessed fellow!

DAD, THE PREACHER
White House, Oct. 2, 1903.

Dear Kermit:

I was very glad to get your letter. Am glad you are playing football. I should be very sorry to see either you or Ted devoting most of your attention to athletics, and I haven't got any special ambition to see you shine overmuch in athletics at college, at least (if you go there), because I think it tends to take up too much time; but I do like to feel that you are manly and able to hold your own in rough, hardy sports. I would rather have a boy of mine stand high in his studies than high in athletics, but I could a great deal rather have him show true manliness of character than show either intellectual or physical prowess; and I believe you and Ted both bid fair to develop just such character.

There! you will think this a dreadfully preaching letter! I suppose I have a natural tendency to preach just at present because I am overwhelmed with my work. I enjoy being

President, and I like to do the work and have my hand on the lever. But it is very worrying and puzzling, and I have to make up my mind to accept every kind of attack and misrepresentation. It is a great comfort to me to read the life and letters of Abraham Lincoln. I am more and more impressed every day, not only with the man's wonderful power and sagacity, but with his literally endless patience, and at the same time his unflinching resolution.

READING UNCLE REMUS
White House, Oct. 19, 1903.

Dear Kermit:

I was much pleased at your being made captain of your eleven. I would rather have you captain of the third eleven than playing on the second.

Yesterday afternoon Ethel on Wyoming, Mother on Yagenka and I on Renown had a long ride, the only incident being meeting a large red automobile, which much shook Renown's nerves, although he behaved far better than he has hitherto been doing about automobiles. In fact, he behaved so well that I leaned over and gave him a lump of sugar when he had passed the object of terror—the old boy eagerly turning his head around to get it. It was lovely out in the country, with the trees at their very best of the fall coloring. There are no red maples here, but the Virginia creepers and some of the dogwoods give the red, and the hickories, tulip trees and beeches a brilliant yellow, sometimes almost orange.

When we got home Mother went up-stairs first and was met by Archie and Quentin, each loaded with pillows and whispering not to let me know that they were in ambush; then as I marched up to the top they assailed me with shrieks and chuckles of delight and then the pillow fight raged up and down the hall. After my bath I read them from Uncle Remus. Usually Mother reads them, but now and then, when I think she really must have a holiday from it, I read them myself.

PONIES AND THE PANAMA CANAL
White House, Oct. 24, 1903.

Dear Kermit:

Yesterday I felt rather seedy, having a touch of Cuban fever, my only unpleasant reminiscence of the Santiago campaign. Accordingly, I spent the afternoon in the house lying on the sofa, with a bright fire burning and Mother in the rocking-chair, with her knitting, beside me. I felt so glad that I was not out somewhere in the wilderness, campaigning or hunting, where I would have to walk or ride all day in the rain and then lie out under a bush at night!

When Allan will come from the trainer's I do not know. Rather to my surprise, Ronald has won golden opinions and really is a very nice dog. Pinckney loves him, and he sits up in the express wagon just as if it was what he had been born to.

Quentin is learning to ride the pony. He had one tumble, which, he remarked philosophically, did not hurt him any more than when I whacked him with a sofa cushion in one of our pillow fights. I think he will very soon be able to manage the pony by himself.

Mother has just taken the three children to spend the afternoon at Dr. Rixey's farm. I am hard at work on my message to Congress, and accordingly shall not try to go out or see any one either this afternoon or this evening. All of this work is terribly puzzling at times, but I peg away at it, and every now and then, when the dust clears away and I look around, I feel that I really have accomplished a little, at any rate.

I think you stood well in your form, taking everything into account. I feel you deserve credit for being captain of your football eleven, and yet standing as high as you do in your class.

SONS TRUMP MESSAGE TO CONGRESS
White House, Nov. 4, 1903.

Dear Kermit:

Tonight while I was preparing to dictate a message to Congress concerning the boiling caldron on the Isthmus of Panama, which has now begun to bubble over, up came one of the ushers with a telegram from you and Ted about the football match. Instantly I bolted into the next room to read it aloud to mother and sister, and we all cheered in unison when we came to the Rah! Rah! Rah! part of it. It was a great score. I wish I could have seen the game.

DAILY BIBLE READINGS
White House, Nov. 15, 1903.

Dear Kermit:

Didn't I tell you about Hector, Brier and Sailor Boy (dogs) when I saw them on election day? They were in excellent health, lying around the door of Seaman's house, which they had evidently adopted as their own. Sailor Boy and Brier were exceedingly affectionate; Hector kindly, but uninterested.

Mother has gone off for nine days, and as usual I am acting as vice-mother. Archie and Quentin are really too cunning for anything. Each night I spend about three-quarters of an hour reading to them. I first of all read some book like Algonquin Indian Tales, or the poetry of Scott or Macaulay. Once I read them Jim Bludsoe, which perfectly enthralled them and made Quentin ask me at least a hundred questions, including one as to whether the colored boy did not find sitting on the safety valve hot. I have also been reading them each evening from the Bible. It has been the story of Saul, David and Jonathan. They have been so interested that several times I have had to read them more than one chapter. Then each says his prayers and repeats the hymn he is learning, Quentin usually jigging solemnly up and down while he repeats it. Each finally got one hymn perfect, whereupon in accordance with previous instructions from mother I presented each of them with a five-cent piece. Yesterday (Saturday) I took both of them and Ethel, together with the three elder Garfield boys, for a long scramble down Rock Creek. We really had great fun.

QUENTIN TURNS SIX
White House, Nov. 19, 1903.

Dear Kermit:

I was much pleased at your being chosen captain of the Seventh. I had not expected it. I rather suspect that you will be behind in your studies this month. If so, try to make up next month, and keep above the middle of the class if you can. I am interested in what you tell me about the Sir Galahads, and I shall want to talk to you about them when you come on.

Mother is back with Aunt Emily, who looks very well. It is so nice to have her. As for Mother, of course she makes the house feel like a home again, instead of like a temporary dwelling.

Leo is as cunning as ever. Pinckney went to see Allan yesterday and said he found him "as busy as a bee in a tar barrel," and evidently owning all the trainer's house. He is not yet quite fit to come back here.

To-day is Quentin's birthday. He has a cold, so he had his birthday cake, with the six candles, and his birthday ice-cream, in the nursery, with Ethel, Archie, Mother, Aunt Emily, myself, Mame and Georgette as admiring guests and onlookers.

A President's Poor Protection
White House, Nov. 28, 1903.

Dear Kermit:

It was very sad at Uncle Gracie's funeral; and yet lovely, too, in a way, for not only all his old friends had turned out, but all of the people connected with the institutions for which he had worked during so many years also came. There were a good many of the older boys and employees from the Newsboys' Lodging House and the Orthopædic Dispensary, etc. Uncle Jimmy possessed a singularly loving and affectionate nature, and I never knew any one who in doing good was more careful to do it unostentatiously. I had no idea how much he had done. Mother with her usual thoughtfulness had kept him steadily in mind while I have been Governor and President; and I now find that he appreciated her so much, her constant remembrances in having him on to visit us on different occasions. It was a lesson to me, for I should probably never have thought of it myself; and of course when one does not do what one ought to, the excuse that one erred from thoughtlessness instead of wrong purpose is of small avail.

The police arrangements at the church were exasperating to a degree. There were fully five hundred policemen in the streets round about, just as if there was danger of an attack by a ferocious mob; and yet though they had throngs of policemen inside, too, an elderly and harmless crank actually got inside with them to present me some foolish memorial about curing the German Emperor from cancer. Inasmuch as what we needed was, not protection against a mob, but a sharp lookout for cranks, the arrangement ought by rights to have been for fifty policemen outside and two or three good detectives inside. I felt like a fool with all the policemen in solemn and purposeless lines around about; and then I felt half exasperated and half amused when I found that they were utterly helpless to prevent a crank from getting inside after all.

P. S. I enclose two original poems by Nick and Archie. They refer to a bit of unhappy advice I gave them, because of which I fell into richly merited disgrace with Mother. Nick has been spending three days or so with Archie, and I suggested that they should explore the White House in the mirk of midnight. They did, in white sheets, and, like little jacks, barefooted. Send me back the poems.

THE FUNERAL OF PETER RABBIT
White House, May 28, 1904.

Dear Kermit:

It was great fun seeing you and Ted, and I enjoyed it to the full. Ethel, Archie and Quentin have gone to Mount Vernon to-day with the Garfield boys. Yesterday poor Peter Rabbit died and his funeral was held with proper state. Archie, in his overalls, dragged the wagon with the little black coffin in which poor Peter Rabbit lay. Mother walked behind as chief mourner, she and Archie solemnly exchanging tributes to the worth and good qualities of the departed. Then he was buried, with a fuchsia over the little grave.

You remember Kenneth Grahame's account of how Harold went to the circus and sang the great spheral song of the circus? Well, yesterday Mother leaned out of her window and heard Archie, swinging under a magnolia tree, singing away to himself, "I'm going to Sagamore, to Sagamore, to Sagamore. I'm going to Sagamore, oh, to Sagamore!" It was his spheral song of joy and thanksgiving.

The children's delight at going to Sagamore next week has completely swallowed up all regret at leaving Mother and me. Quentin is very cunning. He and Archie love to play the hose into the sandbox and then, with their thigh rubber boots on, to get in and make fortifications. Now and then they play it over each other. Ethel is playing tennis quite a good deal.

I think Yagenka is going to come out all right, and Bleistein, too. I have no hope for Wyoming or Renown. Fortunately, Rusty is serving us well.

On the Eve of Nonimation
White House, June 21, 1904.

Dear Kermit:

We spent to-day at the Knoxes'. It is a beautiful farm-just such a one as you could run. Phil Knox, as capable and efficient as he is diminutive, amused Mother and me greatly by the silent way in which he did in first-rate way his full share of all the work.

To-morrow the National Convention meets, and barring a cataclysm I shall be nominated. There is a great deal of sullen grumbling, but it has taken more the form of resentment against what they think is my dictation as to details than against me personally. They don't dare to oppose me for the nomination and I suppose it is hardly likely the attempt will be made to stampede the Convention for any one. How the election will turn out no man can tell. Of course I hope to be elected, but I realize to the full how very lucky I have been, not only to be President but to have been able to accomplish so much while President, and whatever may be the outcome, I am not only content but very sincerely thankful for all the good fortune I have had. From Panama down I have been able to accomplish certain things which will be of lasting importance in our history. Incidentally, I don't think that any family has ever enjoyed the White House more than we have. I was thinking about it just this morning when Mother and I took breakfast on the portico and afterwards walked about the lovely grounds and looked at the stately historic old house. It is a wonderful privilege to have been here and to have been given the chance to do this work, and I should regard myself as having a small and mean mind if in the event of defeat I felt soured at not having had more instead of being thankful for having had so much.

READING *Last of the Mohicans*
White House, Dec. 17, 1904.

Blessed Kermit:

For a week the weather has been cold—down to zero at night and rarely above freezing in the shade at noon. In consequence the snow has lain well, and as there has been a waxing moon I have had the most delightful evening and night rides imaginable. I have been so busy that I have been unable to get away until after dark, but I went in the fur jacket Uncle Will presented to me as the fruit of his prize money in the Spanish War; and the moonlight on the glittering snow made the rides lovelier than they would have been in the daytime. Sometimes Mother and Ted went with me, and the gallops were delightful. To-day it has snowed heavily again, but the snow has been so soft that I did not like to go out, and besides I have been worked up to the limit. There has been skating and sleigh-riding all the week.

The new black "Jack" dog is becoming very much at home and very fond of the family.

With Archie and Quentin I have finished "The Last of the Mohicans," and have now begun "The Deerslayer." They are as cunning as ever, and this reading to them in the evening gives me a chance to see them that I would not otherwise have, although sometimes it is rather hard to get time.

Mother looks very young and pretty. This afternoon she was most busy, taking the little boys to the theatre and then going to hear Ethel sing. Ted, very swell in his first tail coat, is going out to take supper at Secretary Morton's, whose pretty daughter is coming out tonight.

In a very few days now we shall see you again.

AFTER CHURCH MEETINGS
White House, March 20, 1905.

Dear Kermit:

Poor John Hay has been pretty sick. He is going away to try to pick up his health by a sea voyage and rest. I earnestly hope he succeeds, not only because of my great personal fondness for him, but because from the standpoint of the nation it would be very difficult to replace him. Every Sunday on my way home from church I have been accustomed to stop in and see him. The conversation with him was always delightful, and during these Sunday morning talks we often decided important questions of public policy.

I paid a scuttling visit to New York on Friday to give away Eleanor at her marriage, and to make two speeches-one to the Friendly Sons of St. Patrick and one to the Sons of the American Revolution.

Mother and I have been riding a good deal, and the country is now lovely. Moreover, Ted and Matt and I have begun playing tennis.

The birds have come back. Not only song-sparrows and robins, but a winter wren, purple finches and tufted titmice are singing in the garden; and the other morning early Mother and I were waked up by the loud singing of a cardinal bird in the magnolia tree just outside our windows.

Yesterday afternoon Archie and Quentin each had a little boy to see him. They climbed trees, sailed boats in the fountain, and dug in the sand-box like woodcocks.

Poor Mr. Frank Travers died last night. I was very sorry. He has been a good friend to me.

Encouragement to Succeed
White House, Feb. 24, 1905.

Darling Kermit:

I puzzled a good deal over your marks. I am inclined to think that one explanation is that you have thought so much of home as to prevent your really putting your whole strength into your studies. It is most natural that you should count the days before coming home, and write as you do that it will only be 33 days, only 26 days, only 19 days, etc., but at the same time it seems to me that perhaps this means that you do not really put all your heart and all your head effort into your work; and that if you are able to, it would be far better to think just as little as possible about coming home and resolutely set yourself to putting your best thought into your work. It is an illustration of the old adage about putting your hand to the plow and then looking back. In after life, of course, it is always possible that at some time you may have to go away for a year or two from home to do some piece of work. If during that whole time you only thought day after day of how soon you would get home I think you would find it difficult to do your best work; and maybe this feeling may be partly responsible for the trouble with the lessons at school.

Wednesday, Washington's Birthday, I went to Philadelphia and made a speech at the University of Pennsylvania, took lunch with the Philadelphia City Troop and came home the same afternoon with less fatigue than most of my trips cost me; for I was able to dodge the awful evening banquet and the night on the train which taken together drive me nearly melancholy mad. Since Sunday we have not been able to ride. I still box with Grant, who has now become the champion middleweight wrestler of the United States. Yesterday afternoon we had Professor Yamashita up here to wrestle with Grant. It was very interesting, but of course jiu jitsu and our wrestling are so far apart that it is difficult to make any comparison between them. Wrestling is simply a sport with rules almost as conventional as those of tennis, while jiu jitsu is really meant for practice in killing or disabling our adversary. In consequence, Grant did not know what to do except to put Yamashita on his back, and Yamashita was perfectly content to be on his back. Inside of a minute Yamashita had choked Grant, and inside of two minutes more he got an elbow hold on him that would have enabled him to break his arm; so that there is no question but that he could have put Grant out. So far this made it evident that the jiu jitsu man could handle the ordinary wrestler. But Grant, in the actual wrestling and throwing was about as good as the Japanese, and he was so much stronger that he evidently hurt and wore out the Japanese. With a little practice in the art I am sure that one of our big wrestlers or boxers, simply because of his greatly superior strength, would be able to kill any of those Japanese, who though very good men for their inches and pounds are altogether too small to hold their own against big, powerful, quick men who are as well trained.

TEN BEAR AND THREE BOBCATS
Glenwood Springs, Colorado, May 2, 1905.

Blessed Kermit:

I was delighted to get your letter. I am sorry you are having such a hard time in mathematics, but hope a couple of weeks will set you all right. We have had a very successful hunt. All told we have obtained ten bear and three bobcats. Dr. Lambert has been a perfect trump. He is in the pink of condition, while for the last week I have been a little knocked out by the Cuban fever. Up to that time I was simply in splendid shape. There is a very cunning little dog named Skip, belonging to John Goff's pack, who has completely adopted me. I think I shall take him home to Archie. He likes to ride on Dr. Lambert's horse, or mine, and though he is not as big as Jack, takes eager part in the fight with every bear and bobcat.

I am sure you will enjoy your trip to Deadwood with Seth Bullock, and as soon as you return from Groton I shall write to him about it. I have now become very homesick for Mother, and shall be glad when the 12th of May comes and I am back in the White House.

Homesick Dad
White House, May 14, 1905.

Dear Kermit:

Here I am back again, and mighty glad to be back. It was perfectly delightful to see Mother and the children, but it made me very homesick for you. Of course I was up to my ears in work as soon as I reached the White House, but in two or three days we shall be through it and can settle down into our old routine.

Yesterday afternoon we played tennis, Herbert Knox Smith and I beating Matt and Murray. To-day I shall take cunning mother out for a ride.

Skip accompanied me to Washington. He is not as yet entirely at home in the White House and rather clings to my companionship. I think he will soon be fond of Archie, who loves him dearly. Mother is kind to Skip, but she does not think he is an aristocrat as Jack is. He is a very cunning little dog all the same.

Mother walked with me to church this morning and both the past evenings we have been able to go out into the garden and sit on the stone benches near the fountain. The country is too lovely for anything, everything being a deep, rich, fresh green.

I had a great time in Chicago with the labor union men. They made what I regarded as a rather insolent demand upon me, and I gave them some perfectly straight talk about their duty and about the preservation of law and order. The trouble seems to be increasing there, and I may have to send Federal troops into the city—though I shall not do so unless it is necessary.

WELL DONE, SON!
White House, May 14, 1905.

Dear Kermit:

That was a good mark in Latin, and I am pleased with your steady improvement in it.

Skip is housebroken, but he is like a real little Indian. He can stand any amount of hard work if there is a bear or bobcat ahead, but now that he is in the White House he thinks he would much rather do nothing but sit about all day with his friends, and threatens to turn into a lapdog. But when we get him to Oyster Bay I think we can make him go out riding with us, and then I think he will be with Archie a great deal. He and Jack are rather jealous of one another. He is very cunning and friendly. I am immensely pleased with Mother's Virginia cottage and its name. I am going down there for Sunday with her some time soon.

P. S. Your marks have just come! By George, you have worked hard and I am delighted. Three cheers!

COOKING AND TREATIES
White House, June 11, 1905.

Dear Kermit:

Mother and I have just come home from a lovely trip to
"Pine Knot." It is really a perfectly delightful little place;
the nicest little place of the kind you can imagine. Mother
is a great deal more pleased with it than any child with any
toy I ever saw. She went down the day before, Thursday,
and I followed on Friday morning. Good Mr. Joe Wilmer
met me at the station and we rode on horseback to "Round
Top," where we met Mother and Mr. Willie Wilmer. We all
had tea there and then drove to "Plain Dealing," where we
had dinner. Of course I loved both "Round Top" and "Plain
Dealing," and as for the two Mr. Wilmers, they are the
most generous, thoughtful, self-effacing friends that any
one could wish to see. After dinner we went over to "Pine
Knot," put everything to order and went to bed. Next day
we spent all by ourselves at "Pine Knot." In the morning I
fried bacon and eggs, while Mother boiled the kettle for tea
and laid the table. Breakfast was most successful, and then
Mother washed the dishes and did most of the work, while
I did odd jobs. Then we walked about the place, which is
fifteen acres in all, saw the lovely spring, admired the pine
trees and the oak trees, and then Mother lay in the
hammock while I cut away some trees to give us a better
view from the piazza. The piazza is the real feature of the
house. It is broad and runs along the whole length and the
roof is high near the wall, for it is a continuation of the roof
of the house. It was lovely to sit there in the rocking-chairs

and hear all the birds by daytime and at night the whippoorwills and owls and little forest folk.

Inside the house is just a bare wall with one big room below, which is nice now, and will be still nicer when the chimneys are up and there is a fireplace in each end. A rough flight of stairs leads above, where there are two rooms, separated by a passageway. We did everything for ourselves, but all the food we had was sent over to us by the dear Wilmers, together with milk. We cooked it ourselves, so there was no one around the house to bother us at all. As we found that cleaning dishes took up an awful time we only took two meals a day, which was all we wanted. On Saturday evening I fried two chickens for dinner, while Mother boiled the tea, and we had cherries and wild strawberries, as well as biscuits and cornbread. To my pleasure Mother greatly enjoyed the fried chicken and admitted that what you children had said of the way I fried chicken was all true. In the evening we sat out a long time on the piazza, and then read indoors and then went to bed. Sunday morning we did not get up until nine. Then I fried Mother some beefsteak and some eggs in two frying-pans, and she liked them both very much. We went to church at the dear little church where the Wilmers' father and mother had been married, dined soon after two at "Plain Dealing," and then were driven over to the station to go back to Washington. I rode the big black stallion—Chief—and enjoyed it thoroughly. Altogether we had a very nice holiday.

I was lucky to be able to get it, for during the past fortnight, and indeed for a considerable time before, I have been carrying on negotiations with both Russia and Japan, together with side negotiations with Germany, France and England, to try to get the present war stopped. With infinite labor and by the exercise of a good deal of tact and judgment—if I do say it myself—I have finally gotten the Japanese and Russians to agree to meet to discuss the terms of peace. Whether they will be able to come to an agreement or not I can't say. But it is worth while to have obtained the chance of peace, and the only possible way to get this chance was to secure such an agreement of the two powers that they would meet and discuss the terms direct. Of course Japan will want to ask more than she ought to ask, and Russia to give less than she ought to give. Perhaps both sides will prove impracticable. Perhaps one will. But there is the chance that they will prove sensible, and make a peace, which will really be for the interest of each as things are now. At any rate the experiment was worth trying. I have kept the secret very successfully, and my dealings with the Japanese in particular have been known to no one, so that the result is in the nature of a surprise.

PUNKEY, DOODLE, AND JOLLAPIN
Oyster Bay, N. Y., Aug. 26, 1905.

Dear Kermit:

Mr. Phil Stewart and Dr. Lambert spent a night here, Quentin greeting the former with most cordial friendship, and in explanation stating that he always liked to get acquainted with everybody. I take Hall to chop, and he plays tennis with Phil and Oliver, and rides with Phil and Quentin.

The Plunger (a submarine) has come to the Bay and I am going out in it this afternoon-or rather down on it. N. B.—I have just been down, for 50 minutes; it was very interesting.

Last night I listened to Mother reading "The Lances of Linwood" to the two little boys and then hearing them their prayers. Then I went into Archie's room, where they both showed all their china animals; I read them Laura E. Richards' poems, including "How does the President take his tea?" They christened themselves Punkey Doodle and Jollapin, from the chorus of this, and immediately afterwards I played with them on Archie's bed. First I would toss Punkey Doodle (Quentin) on Jollapin (Archie) and tickle Jollapin while Punkey Doodle squalled and wiggled on top of him, and then reverse them and keep Punkey Doodle down by heaving Jollapin on him, while they both kicked and struggled until my shirt front looked very much the worse for wear. You doubtless remember yourself how bad it was for me, when I was dressed for dinner, to play with all you scamps when you were little.

The other day a reporter asked Quentin something about me; to which that affable and canny young gentleman responded, "Yes, I see him sometimes; but I know nothing of his family life."

VISITS WITH PRINCES
White House, November 6, 1905.

Dear Kermit:

Just a line, for I really have nothing to say this week. I have caught up with my work. One day we had a rather forlorn little poet and his nice wife in at lunch. They made me feel quite badly by being so grateful at my having mentioned him in what I fear was a very patronizing and, indeed, almost supercilious way, as having written an occasional good poem. I am much struck by Robinson's two poems which you sent Mother. What a queer, mystical creature he is! I did not understand one of them-that about the gardens-and I do not know that I like either of them quite as much as some of those in "The Children of the Night." But he certainly has got the real spirit of poetry in him. Whether he can make it come out I am not quite sure.

Prince Louis of Battenberg has been here and I have been very much pleased with him. He is a really good admiral, and in addition he is a well-read and cultivated man and it was charming to talk with him. We had him and his nephew, Prince Alexander, a midshipman, to lunch alone with us, and we really enjoyed having them. At the State dinner he sat between me and Bonaparte, and I could not help smiling to myself in thinking that here was this British Admiral seated beside the American Secretary of the Navy-the American Secretary of the Navy being the grandnephew of Napoleon and the grandson of Jerome, King of Westphalia; while the British Admiral was the grandson of a

Hessian general who was the subject of King Jerome and served under Napoleon, and then, by no means creditably, deserted him in the middle of the Battle of Leipsic.

I am off to vote tonight.

DUTY REQUIRES MANHOOD
White House, November 19, 1905.

Dear Kermit:

I sympathize with every word you say in your letter, about Nicholas Nickleby, and about novels generally. Normally I only care for a novel if the ending is good, and I quite agree with you that if the hero has to die he ought to die worthily and nobly, so that our sorrow at the tragedy shall be tempered with the joy and pride one always feels when a man does his duty well and bravely. There is quite enough sorrow and shame and suffering and baseness in real life, and there is no need for meeting it unnecessarily in fiction. As Police Commissioner it was my duty to deal with all kinds of squalid misery and hideous and unspeakable infamy, and I should have been worse than a coward if I had shrunk from doing what was necessary; but there would have been no use whatever in my reading novels detailing all this misery and squalor and crime, or at least in reading them as a steady thing. Now and then there is a powerful but sad story which really is interesting and which really does good; but normally the books which do good and the books which healthy people find interesting are those which are not in the least of the sugar-candy variety, but which, while portraying foulness and suffering when they must be portrayed, yet have a joyous as well as a noble side.

We have had a very mild and open fall. I have played tennis a good deal, the French Ambassador being now quite a steady playmate, as he and I play about alike; and I have ridden with Mother a great deal. Last Monday when Mother had gone to New York I had Selous, the great African hunter, to spend the day and night. He is a perfect old dear; just as simple and natural as can be and very interesting. I took him, with Bob Bacon, Gifford Pinchot, Ambassador Meyer and Jim Garfield, for a good scramble and climb in the afternoon, and they all came to dinner afterwards. Before we came down to dinner I got him to spend three-quarters of an hour in telling delightfully exciting lion and hyena stories to Ethel, Archie and Quentin. He told them most vividly and so enthralled the little boys that the next evening I had to tell them a large number myself.

To-day is Quentin's birthday and he loved his gifts, perhaps most of all the weest, cunningest live pig you ever saw, presented him by Straus. Phil Stewart and his wife and boy, Wolcott (who is Archie's age), spent a couple of nights here. One afternoon we had hide-and-go-seek, bringing down Mr. Garfield and the Garfield boys, and Archie turning up with the entire football team, who took a day off for the special purpose. We had obstacle races, hide-and-go-seek, blind-man's buff, and everything else; and there were times when I felt that there was a perfect shoal of small boys bursting in every direction up and down stairs, and through and over every conceivable object.

Mother and I still walk around the grounds every day after breakfast. The gardens, of course, are very, very dishevelled now, the snap-dragons holding out better than any other flowers.

Books and Such
White House, February 3, 1906.

Dear Kermit:

I agree pretty well with your views of David Copperfield. Dora was very cunning and attractive, but I am not sure that the husband would retain enough respect for her to make life quite what it ought to be with her. This is a harsh criticism and I have known plenty of women of the Dora type whom I have felt were a good deal better than the men they married, and I have seen them sometimes make very happy homes. I also feel as you do that if a man had to struggle on and make his way it would be a great deal better to have some one like Sophie. Do you recollect that dinner at which David Copperfield and Traddles were, where they are described as seated at the dinner, one "in the glare of the red velvet lady" and the other "in the gloom of Hamlet's aunt?" I am so glad you like Thackeray. "Pendennis" and "The Newcomes" and "Vanity Fair" I can read over and over again.

Ted blew in today. I think he has been studying pretty well this term and now he is through all his examinations but one. He hopes, and I do, that you will pay what attention you can to athletics. Play hockey, for instance, and try to get into shape for the mile run. I know it is too short a distance for you, but if you will try for the hare and hounds running and the mile, too, you may be able to try for the two miles when you go to Harvard.

The weather was very mild early in the week. It has turned cold now; but Mother and I had a good ride yesterday, and Ted and I a good ride this afternoon, Ted on Grey Dawn. We have been having a perfect whirl of dinner engagements; but thank heavens they will stop shortly after Sister's wedding.

ARCHIES SAVES A BOY'S SIGHT
White House, March 11, 1906.

Dear Kermit:

I agree pretty much to all your views both about Thackeray and Dickens, although you care for some of Thackeray of which I am not personally fond. Mother loves it all. Mother, by the way, has been reading "The Legend of Montrose" to the little boys and they are absorbed in it. She finds it hard to get anything that will appeal to both Archie and Quentin, as they possess such different natures.

I am quite proud of what Archie did the day before yesterday. Some of the bigger boys were throwing a baseball around outside of Mr. Sidwell's school and it hit one of them square in the eye, breaking all the blood-vessels and making an extremely dangerous hurt. The other boys were all rattled and could do nothing, finally sneaking off when Mr. Sidwell appeared. Archie stood by and himself promptly suggested that the boy should go to Dr. Wilmer. Accordingly he scorched down to Dr. Wilmer's and said there was an emergency case for one of Mr. Sidwell's boys, who was hurt in the eye, and could he bring him. Dr. Wilmer, who did not know Archie was there, sent out word to of course do so. So Archie scorched back on his wheel, got the boy (I do not know why Mr. Sidwell did not take him himself) and led him down to Dr. Wilmer's, who attended to his eye and had to send him at once to a hospital, Archie waiting until he heard the result and then coming home. Dr. Wilmer told me about it and said if Archie had not acted with such promptness the boy (who was four or five years older than Archie, by the way) would have lost his sight.

What a heavenly place a sandbox is for two little boys! Archie and Quentin play industriously in it during most of their spare moments when out in the grounds. I often look out of the office windows when I have a score of Senators and Congressmen with me and see them both hard at work arranging caverns or mountains, with runways for their marbles.

Good-bye, blessed fellow. I shall think of you very often during the coming week, and I am so very glad that Mother is to be with you at your confirmation.

PILLOW FIGHTS WITH THE BOYS
White House, March 19, 1906.

Darling Kermit:

During the four days Mother was away I made a point of seeing the children each evening for three-quarters of an hour or so. Archie and Quentin are really great playmates. One night I came up-stairs and found Quentin playing the pianola as hard as he could, while Archie would suddenly start from the end of the hall where the pianola was, and, accompanied by both the dogs, race as hard as he could the whole length of the White House clean to the other end of the hall and then tear back again. Another evening as I came up-stairs I found Archie and Quentin having a great play, chuckling with laughter, Archie driving Quentin by his suspenders, which were fixed to the end of a pair of woollen reins. Then they would ambush me and we would have a vigorous pillow-fight, and after five or ten minutes of this we would go into Mother's room, and I would read them the book Mother had been reading them, "The Legend of Montrose." We just got through it the very last evening. Both Skip and Jack have welcomed Mother back with frantic joy, and this morning came in and lay on her bed as soon as she had finished breakfast—for she did not come down to either breakfast or lunch, as she is going to spend the night at Baltimore with the Bonapartes.

I was so interested in your reading "Phineas Finn" that I ordered a copy myself. I have also ordered DeQuincey's works, as I find we have not got them at the White House.

PLAYING "TICKLEY"
White House, April 12, 1906.

Dear Kermit:

Last night I played "tickley" in their room with the two little boys. As we rolled and bounced over all three beds in the course of the play, not to mention frantic chases under them, I think poor Mademoiselle was rather appalled at the result when we had finished. Archie's seven-weeks-old St. Bernard puppy has come and it is the dearest puppy imaginable; a huge, soft thing, which Archie carries around in his arms and which the whole family loves.

Yesterday I took a first ride on the new horse, Roswell, Captain Lee going along on Rusty as a kind of a nurse. Roswell is not yet four and he is really a green colt and not quite the horse I want at present, as I haven't time to fuss with him, and am afraid of letting the Sergeant ride him, as he does not get on well with him, and there is nobody else in our stable that can ride at all. He is a beautiful horse, a wonderful jumper, and does not pull at all. He shies pretty badly, especially when he meets an automobile; and when he leaves the stable or strikes a road that he thinks will take him home and is not allowed to go down it, he is apt to rear, which I do not like; but I am inclined to think that he will get over these traits, and if I can arrange to have Lee handle him a couple of months more, and if Ted and I can regularly ride him down at Oyster Bay, I think that he will turn out all right.

Mother and I walk every morning through the grounds, which, of course, are lovely. Not only are the song-sparrows and robins singing, but the white-throated sparrows, who will, I suppose, soon leave us for the North, are still in full song, and this morning they waked us up at daybreak singing just outside the window.

DISCUSSING CURRENT EVENTS
White House, April 22, 1906.

Dear Kermit:

Ted has been as good and cunning as possible. He has completely recovered from the effects of having his eye operated upon, and though the eye itself is a somewhat gruesome object, Ted is in the highest spirits. He goes back to Harvard today.

As I write, Archie and Quentin are busily engaged in the sand-box and I look out across the tennis-ground at them. If ever there was a heaven-sent treasure to small boys, that sand-box is the treasure. It was very cunning to see the delight various little children took in it at the egg-rolling on Easter Monday. Thanks to our decision in keeping out grown people and stopping everything at one o'clock, the egg-rolling really was a children's festival, and was pretty and not objectionable this year.

The apple trees are now coming into bloom, including that big arched apple tree, under which Mother and I sit, by the fountain, on the stone bench. It is the apple tree that Mother particularly likes....

Did Quentin write his poems after you had gone? I

never can recollect whether you have seen them or not. He is a funny small person if ever there was one. The other day we were discussing a really dreadful accident which had happened; a Georgetown young man having taken out a young girl in a canoe on the river, the canoe upset and the girl was drowned; whereupon the young man, when he got home, took what seemed to us an exceedingly cold-blooded method of a special delivery letter to notify her parents. We were expressing our horror at his sending a special delivery letter, and Quentin solemnly chimed in with "Yes, he wasted ten cents." There was a moment's eloquent silence, and then we strove to explain to Quentin that what we were objecting to was not in the least the young man's spendthrift attitude!

As I walk to and from the office now the terrace is fairly fragrant with the scent of the many-colored hyacinths which Mother has put out in boxes on the low stone walls.

A Visit to Washington's Birthplace
White House, April 30, 1906.

Dear Kermit:

On Saturday afternoon Mother and I started off on the Slyph, Mother having made up her mind I needed thirty-six hours' rest, and we had a delightful time together, and she was just as cunning as she could be. On Sunday Mother and I spent about four hours ashore, taking our lunch and walking up to the monument which marks where the house stood in which Washington was born. It is a simple shaft. Every vestige of the house is destroyed, but a curious and rather pathetic thing is that, although it must be a hundred years since the place was deserted, there are still multitudes of flowers which must have come from those in the old garden. There are iris and narcissus and a little blue flower, with a neat, prim, clean smell that makes one feel as if it ought to be put with lavender into chests of fresh old linen. The narcissus in particular was growing around everywhere, together with real wild flowers like the painted columbine and star of Bethlehem. It was a lovely spot on a headland overlooking a broad inlet from the Potomac. There was also the old graveyard or grave plot in which were the gravestones of Washington's father and mother and grandmother, all pretty nearly ruined. It was lovely warm weather and Mother and I enjoyed our walk through the funny lonely old country. Mocking-birds, meadow-larks, Carolina wrens, cardinals, and field sparrows were singing cheerfully. We came up the river in time to get home last evening. This morning Mother and I walked around the White House grounds as usual. I think I get more fond of flowers every year. The grounds are now at that high stage of beauty in which they will stay for the next two months. The buckeyes are in bloom, the pink dogwood, and the fragrant lilacs, which are almost the loveliest of the bushes; and then the flowers, including the lily-of-the-valley.

I am dictating in the office. Archie is out by the sandbox playing with the hose. The playing consists in brandishing it around his head and trying to escape the falling water. He escapes about twice out of three times and must now be a perfect drowned rat. (I have just had him in to look at him and he is even more of a drowned rat than I supposed. He has gone out to complete his shower bath under strict promise that immediately afterwards he will go in and change his clothes.)

Quentin is the funniest mite you ever saw and certainly a very original little fellow. He left at Mademoiselle's plate yesterday a large bunch of flowers with the inscription that they were from the fairies to her to reward her for taking care of "two good, good boys." Ethel is a dear.

SAILING AND ROWING
Oyster Bay, Aug. 18, 1906.

Dear Kermit:

Quentin is the same cheerful pagan philosopher as ever. He swims like a little duck; rides well; stands quite severe injuries without complaint, and is really becoming a manly little fellow. Archie is devoted to the Why (sailboat). The other day while Mother and I were coming in, rowing, we met him sailing out, and it was too cunning for anything. The Why looks exactly like a little black wooden shoe with a sail in it, and the crew consisted of Archie, of one of his beloved playmates, a seaman from the Sylph, and of Skip-very alert and knowing.

PUPPY DOG GAMES
White House, October 23, 1906.

Dear Kermit:

Archie is very cunning and has handicap races with Skip. He spreads his legs, bends over, and holds Skip between them. Then he says, "On your mark, Skip, ready; go!" and shoves Skip back while he runs as hard as he possibly can to the other end of the hall, Skip scrambling wildly with his paws on the smooth floor until he can get started, when he races after Archie, the object being for Archie to reach the other end before Skip can overtake him.

Happy Hunting
White House, November 4, 1906.

Dear Kermit:

Just a line to tell you what a nice time we had at Pine Knot. Mother was as happy as she always is there, and as cunning and pretty as possible. As for me, I hunted faithfully through all three days, leaving the house at three o'clock one day, at four the next, and at five the next, so that I began my hunts in absolute night; but fortunately we had a brilliant moon on each occasion. The first two days were failures. I did not see a turkey, and on each occasion when everybody was perfectly certain that I was going to see a turkey, something went wrong and the turkey did not turn up. The last day I was out thirteen hours, and you may imagine how hungry I was when I got back, not to speak of being tired; though fortunately most of the time I was rambling around on horseback, so I was not done out. But in the afternoon at last luck changed, and then for once everything went right. The hunter who was with me marked a turkey in a point of pines stretching down from a forest into an open valley, with another forest on its farther side. I ran down to the end of the point and hid behind a bush. He walked down through the pines and the turkey came out and started to fly across the valley, offering me a beautiful side shot at about thirty-five yards—just the distance for my ten-bore. I killed it dead, and felt mighty happy as it came tumbling down through the air.

Your Mother is Beautiful
On Board U. S. S. Louisiana,Nov. 13. 1906

Dear Kermit:

So far this trip has been a great success, and I think Mother has really enjoyed it. As for me, I of course feel a little bored, as I always do on shipboard, but I have brought on a great variety of books, and am at this moment reading Milton's prose works, "Tacitus," and a German novel called "Jorn Uhl." Mother and I walk briskly up and down the deck together, or else sit aft under the awning, or in the after cabin, with the gun ports open, and read; and I also spend a good deal of time on the forward bridge, and sometimes on the aft bridge, and of course have gone over the ship to inspect it with the Captain. It is a splendid thing to see one of these men-of-war, and it does really make one proud of one's country. Both the officers and the enlisted men are as fine a set as one could wish to see.

It is a beautiful sight, these three great war-ships standing southward in close column, and almost as beautiful at night when we see not only the lights but the loom through the darkness of the ships astern. We are now in the tropics and I have thought a good deal of the time over eight years ago when I was sailing to Santiago in the fleet of warships and transports. It seems a strange thing to think of my now being President, going to visit the work of the Panama Canal which I have made possible.

Mother, very pretty and dainty in white summer clothes, came up on Sunday morning to see inspection and review, or whatever they call it, of the men. I usually spend half an hour on deck before Mother is dressed. Then we breakfast together alone; have also taken lunch alone, but at dinner have two or three officers to dine with us. Doctor Rixey is along, and is a perfect dear, as always.

OF KILTS, SONGS, AND HEROES
U. S. S. Louisiana, At Sea, November 23, 1906.

Dear Kermit:

We had a most interesting two days at Porto Rico. We landed on the south side of the island and were received by the Governor and the rest of the administration, including nice Mr. Laurance Grahame; then were given a reception by the Alcalde and people of Ponce; and then went straight across the island in automobiles to San Juan on the north shore. It was an eighty mile trip and really delightful. The road wound up to the high mountains of the middle island, through them, and then down again to the flat plain on the north shore. The scenery was beautiful. It was as thoroughly tropical as Panama but much more livable. There were palms, tree-ferns, bananas, mangoes, bamboos, and many other trees and multitudes of brilliant flowers. There was one vine called the dream-vine with flowers as big as great white water-lilies, which close up tight in the day-time and bloom at night. There were vines with masses of brilliant purple and pink flowers, and others with masses of little white flowers, which at night-time smell deliciously. There were trees studded over with huge white flowers, and others, the flamboyants such as I saw in the campaign at Santiago, are a mass of large scarlet blossoms in June, but which now had shed them. I thought the tree-ferns especially beautiful. The towns were just such as you saw in Cuba, quaint, brilliantly colored, with the old church or cathedral fronting the plaza, and the plaza always full of flowers. Of course the towns are dirty, but they are not nearly as dirty and offensive as those of Italy; and there is something pathetic and childlike about the people. We are giving them a good government and the island is prospering. I never saw a finer set of young fellows than those engaged in the administration. Mr. Grahame, whom of course you remember, is the intimate friend and ally of the leaders of the administration, that is of Governor Beekman Winthrop and of the Secretary of State, Mr. Regis Post. Grahame is a perfect trump and such a handsome, athletic fellow, and a real Sir Galahad. Any wrong-doing, and especially any cruelty makes him flame with fearless indignation. He perfectly delighted the Porto Ricans and also immensely puzzled them by coming in his Scotch kilt to a Government ball. Accordingly, at my special request, I had him wear his kilt at the state dinner and reception the night we were at the palace. You know he is a descendant of Montrose, and although born in Canada, his parents were Scotch and he was educated in Scotland. Do tell Mr. Bob Fergie about him and his kilts when you next write him.

We spent the night at the palace, which is half palace and half castle, and was the residence of the old Spanish governors. It is nearly four hundred years old, and is a delightful building, with quaint gardens and a quaint sea-wall looking over the bay. There were colored lanterns lighting up the gardens for the reception, and the view across the bay in the moonlight was lovely. Our rooms were as attractive as possible too, except that they were so very airy and open that we found it difficult to sleep—not that that much mattered as, thanks to the earliness of our start and the lateness of our reception, we had barely four hours in which we even tried to sleep.

The next morning we came back in automobiles over different and even more beautiful roads. The mountain passes through and over which we went made us feel as if we were in a tropic Switzerland. We had to cross two or three rivers where big cream-colored oxen with yokes tied to their horns pulled the automobiles through the water. At one funny little village we had an open air lunch, very good, of chicken and eggs and bread, and some wine contributed by a wealthy young Spaniard who rode up from a neighboring coffee ranch.

Yesterday afternoon we embarked again, and that evening the crew gave a theatrical entertainment on the afterdeck, closing with three boxing bouts. I send you the program. It was great fun, the audience being equally enraptured with the sentimental songs about the flag, and the sailor's true love and his mother, and with the jokes (the most relished of which related to the fact that bed-bugs were supposed to be so large that they had to be shot!) and the skits about the commissary and various persons and deeds on the ship. In a way the freedom of comment reminded me a little of the Roman triumphs, when the excellent legendaries recited in verse and prose, anything they chose concerning the hero in whose deeds they had shared and whose triumphs they were celebrating. The stage, well lighted, was built on the aftermost part of the deck. We sat in front with the officers, and the sailors behind us in masses on the deck, on the aftermost turrets, on the bridge, and even in the fighting top of the aftermost mast. It was interesting to see their faces in the light.

P. S. I forgot to tell you about the banners and inscriptions of welcome to me in Porto Rico. One of them which stretched across the road had on it "Welcome to Theodore and Mrs. Roosevelt." Last evening I really enjoyed a rather funny experience. There is an Army and Navy Union composed chiefly of enlisted men, but also of many officers, and they suddenly held a "garrison" meeting in the torpedo-room of this ship. There were about fifty enlisted men together with the Captain and myself. I was introduced as "comrade and shipmate Theodore Roosevelt, President of the United States." They were such a nice set of fellows, and I was really so pleased to be with them; so self-respecting, so earnest, and just the right type out of which to make the typical American fighting man who is also a good citizen. The meeting reminded me a good deal of a lodge meeting at Oyster Bay; and of course those men are fundamentally of the same type as the shipwrights, railroad men and fishermen whom I met at the lodge, and who, by the way, are my chief backers politically and are the men who make up the real strength of this nation.

SICKNESS OF ARCHIE
White House, March 3, 1907.

Dear Kermit:

Poor little Archie has diphtheria, and we have had a wearing forty-eight hours. Of course it is harder upon Mother a good deal than upon me, because she spends her whole time with him together with the trained nurse, while I simply must attend to my work during these closing hours of Congress (I have worked each day steadily up to half past seven and also in the evening); and only see Archiekins for twenty minutes or a half hour before dinner. The poor little fellow likes to have me put my hands on his forehead, for he says they smell so clean and soapy! Last night he was very sick, but this morning he is better, and Dr. Rixey thinks everything is going well. Dr. Lambert is coming on this afternoon to see him. Ethel, who is away at Philadelphia, will be sent to stay with the Rixeys. Quentin, who has been exposed somewhat to infection, is not allowed to see other little boys, and is leading a career of splendid isolation among the ushers and policemen.

Since I got back here I have not done a thing except work as the President must during the closing days of a session of Congress. Mother was, fortunately, getting much better, but now of course is having a very hard time of it nursing darling little Archie. He is just as good as gold—so patient and loving. Yesterday that scamp Quentin said to Mademoiselle: "If only I had Archie's nature, and my head, wouldn't it be great?"

In all his sickness Archie remembered that today was Mademoiselle's birthday, and sent her his love and congratulations—which promptly reduced good Mademoiselle to tears.

AT THE JAMESTOWN TRICENTENNIARY
White House, April 29, 1907.

Dearest Kermit:

We really had an enjoyable trip to Jamestown. The guests were Mother's friend, Mrs. Johnson, a Virginia lady who reminds me so much of Aunt Annie, my mother's sister, who throughout my childhood was almost as much associated in our home life as my mother herself; Justice Moody, who was as delightful as he always is, and with whom it was a real pleasure to again have a chance to talk; Mr. and Mrs. Bob Bacon, who proved the very nicest guests of all and were companionable and sympathetic at every point. Ethel was as good as gold and took much off of Mother's shoulders in the way of taking care of Quentin. Archie and Quentin had, of course, a heavenly time; went everywhere, below and aloft, and ate indifferently at all hours, both with the officers and enlisted men. We left here Thursday afternoon, and on Friday morning passed in review through the foreign fleet and our own fleet of sixteen great battleships in addition to cruisers. It was an inspiring sight and one I would not have missed for a great deal. Then we went in a launch to the Exposition where I had the usual experience in such cases, made the usual speech, held the usual reception, went to the usual lunch, etc., etc.

In the evening Mother and I got on the Sylph and went to Norfolk to dine. When the Sylph landed we were met by General Grant to convoy us to the house. I was finishing dressing, and Mother went out into the cabin and sat down to receive him. In a minute or two I came out and began to hunt for my hat. Mother sat very erect and pretty, looking at my efforts with a tolerance that gradually changed to impatience. Finally she arose to get her own cloak, and then I found that she had been sitting gracefully but firmly on the hat herself—it was a crush hat and it had been flattened until it looked like a wrinkled pie. Mother did not see what she had done so I speechlessly thrust the hat toward her; but she still did not understand and took it as an inexplicable jest of mine merely saying, "Yes, dear," and with patient dignity, turned and went out of the door with General Grant.

The next morning we went on the Sylph up the James River, and on the return trip visited three of the dearest places you can imagine, Shirley, Westover, and Brandon. I do not know whether I loved most the places themselves or the quaint out-of-the-world Virginia gentlewomen in them. The houses, the grounds, the owners, all were too dear for anything and we loved them. That night we went back to the Mayflower and returned here yesterday, Sunday, afternoon.

To-day spring weather seems really to have begun, and after lunch Mother and I sat under the apple-tree by the fountain. A purple finch was singing in the apple-tree overhead, and the white petals of the blossoms were silently falling. This afternoon Mother and I are going out riding with Senator Lodge.

THE NAVY KEEPS THE PEACE
White House, May 12, 1907.

Dear Kermit:

General Kuroki and his suite are here and dined with us at a formal dinner last evening. Everything that he says has to be translated, but nevertheless I had a really interesting talk with him, because I am pretty well acquainted with his campaigns. He impressed me much, as indeed all Japanese military and naval officers do. They are a formidable outfit. I want to try to keep on the best possible terms with Japan and never do her any wrong; but I want still more to see our navy maintained at the highest point of efficiency, for it is the real keeper of the peace.

A STEAM WHEELER VOYAGE
On Board U. S. S. Mississippi, October 1, 1907.

Dear Kermit:

After speaking at Keokuk this morning we got aboard this brand new stern-wheel steamer of the regular Mississippi type and started down-stream. I went up in the Texas and of course felt an almost irresistible desire to ask the pilot about Mark Twain. It is a broad, shallow, muddy river, at places the channel being barely wide enough for the boat to go through, though to my inexperienced eyes the whole river looks like a channel. The bottom lands, Illinois on one side and Missouri on the other, are sometimes over-grown with forests and sometimes great rich cornfields, with here and there a house, here and there villages, and now and then a little town. At every such place all the people of the neighborhood have gathered to greet me. The water-front of the towns would be filled with a dense packed mass of men, women, and children, waving flags. The little villages have not only their own population, but also the farmers who have driven in in their wagons with their wives and children from a dozen miles back-just such farmers as came to see you and the cavalry on your march through Iowa last summer.

It is my first trip on the Mississippi, and I am greatly interested in it. How wonderful in its rapidity of movement has been the history of our country, compared with the history of the old world. For untold ages this river had been flowing through the lonely continent, not very greatly changed since the close of the Pleistocene. During all these myriads of years the prairie and the forest came down to its banks. The immense herds of the buffalo and the elk wandered along them season after season, and the Indian hunters on foot or in canoes trudged along the banks or skimmed the water. Probably a thousand years saw no change that would have been noticeable to our eyes. Then three centuries ago began the work of change. For a century its effects were not perceptible. Just nothing but an occasional French fleet or wild half savage French-Canadian explorer passing up or down the river or one of its branches in an Indian canoe; then the first faint changes, the building of one or two little French fur traders' hamlets, the passing of one or two British officers' boats, and the very rare appearance of the uncouth American backwoodsman.

Then the change came with a rush. Our settlers reached the head-waters of the Ohio, and flatboats and keel-boats began to go down to the mouth of the Mississippi, and the Indians and the game they followed began their last great march to the west. For ages they had marched back and forth, but from this march there was never to be a return. Then the day of steamboat traffic began, and the growth of the first American cities and states along the river with their strength and their squalor and their raw pride. Then this mighty steamboat traffic passed its zenith and collapsed, and for a generation the river towns have dwindled compared with the towns which took their importance from the growth of the railroads. I think of it all as I pass down the river.

October 4

We are steaming down the river now between Tennessee and Arkansas. The forest comes down a little denser to the bank, the houses do not look quite so well kept; otherwise there is not much change. There are a dozen steamers accompanying us, filled with delegates from various river cities. The people are all out on the banks to greet us still. Moreover, at night, no matter what the hour is that we pass a town, it is generally illuminated, and sometimes whistles and noisy greetings, while our steamboats whistle in equally noisy response, so that our sleep is apt to be broken. Seventeen governors of different states are along, in a boat by themselves. I have seen a good deal of them, however, and it has been of real use to me, especially as regards two or three problems that are up. At St. Louis there was an enormous multitude of people out to see us. The procession was in a drenching rain, in which I stood bareheaded, smiling affably and waving my drowned hat to those hardy members of the crowd who declined to go to shelter. At Cairo, I was also greeted with great enthusiasm, and I was interested to find that there was still extreme bitterness felt over Dickens's description of the town and the people in "Martin Chuzzlewit" sixty-five years ago.

GOOD READING FOR PACIFISTS
March 4, 1908.

Dearest Kermit:

You have recently been writing me about Dickens. Senator Lodge gave me the following first-class quotation from a piece by Dickens about "Proposals for Amusing Posterity":

"And I would suggest that if a body of gentlemen possessing their full phrenological share of the combative and antagonistic organs, could only be induced to form themselves into a society for Declaiming about Peace, with a very considerable war-whoop against all non-declaimers; and if they could only be prevailed upon to sum up eloquently the many unspeakable miseries and horrors of War, and to present them to their own country as a conclusive reason for its being undefended against War, and becoming a prey of the first despot who might choose to inflict those miseries and horrors—why then I really believe we should have got to the very best joke we could hope to have in our whole Complete Jest-Book for Posterity and might fold our arms and rest convinced that we had done enough for that discerning Patriarch's amusement."

This ought to be read before all the tomfool peace societies and anti-imperialist societies of the present-day.

Skip the Bosh and Twaddle
White House, February 23, 1908.

Dearest Kermit:

I quite agree with you about Tom Pinch. He is a despicable kind of character; just the kind of character Dickens liked, because he had himself a thick streak of maudlin sentimentality of the kind that, as somebody phrased it, "made him wallow naked in the pathetic." It always interests me about Dickens to think how much first-class work he did and how almost all of it was mixed up with every kind of cheap, second-rate matter. I am very fond of him. There are innumerable characters that he has created which symbolize vices, virtues, follies, and the like almost as well as the characters in Bunyan; and therefore I think the wise thing to do is simply to skip the bosh and twaddle and vulgarity and untruth, and get the benefit out of the rest. Of course one fundamental difference between Thackeray and Dickens is that Thackeray was a gentleman and Dickens was not. But a man might do some mighty good work and not be a gentleman in any sense.

Dickens—A Selfish Cad and Boor
White House, February 29, 1908.

Dearest Kermit:

Of course I entirely agree with you about "Martin Chuzzlewit." But the point seems to me that the preposterous perversion of truth and the ill-nature and malice of the book are of consequence chiefly as indicating Dickens' own character, about which I care not a rap; whereas, the characters in American shortcomings, and vices and follies as typified are immortal, and, moreover, can be studied with great profit by all of us today. Dickens was an ill-natured, selfish cad and boor, who had no understanding of what the word gentleman meant, and no appreciation of hospitality or good treatment. He was utterly incapable of seeing the high purpose and the real greatness which (in spite of the presence also of much that was bad or vile) could have been visible all around him here in America to any man whose vision was both keen and lofty. He could not see the qualities of the young men growing up here, though it was these qualities that enabled these men to conquer the West and to fight to a finish the great Civil War, and though they were to produce leadership like that of Lincoln, Lee, and Grant. Naturally he would think there was no gentleman in New York, because by no possibility could he have recognized a gentleman if he had met one. Naturally he would condemn all America because he had not the soul to see what America was really doing. But he was in his element in describing with bitter truthfulness Scadder and Jefferson Brick, and Elijah Pogram, and Hannibal Chollup, and Mrs. Hominy and the various other characters, great and small, that have always made me enjoy "Martin Chuzzlewit." Most of these characters we still have with us.

QUENTIN AND THE PIG
White House, October 17, 1908.

Dearest Kermit:

Quentin performed a characteristic feat yesterday. He heard that Schmidt, the animal man, wanted a small pig, and decided that he would turn an honest penny by supplying the want. So out in the neighborhood of his school he called on an elderly darkey who, he had seen, possessed little pigs; bought one; popped it into a bag; astutely dodged the school—having a well-founded distrust of how the boys would feel toward his passage with the pig—and took the car for home. By that time the pig had freed itself from the bag, and, as he explained, he journeyed in with a "small squealish pig" under his arm; but as the conductor was a friend of his he was not put off. He bought it for a dollar and sold it to Schmidt for a dollar and a quarter, and feels as if he had found a permanent line of business. Schmidt then festooned it in red ribbons and sent it to parade the streets. I gather that Quentin led it around for part of the parade, but he was somewhat vague on this point, evidently being a little uncertain as to our approval of the move.

LETTERS TO
ARCHIE

LIZARD PRESENTS FOR THE BOYS
Del Monte, Cal., May 10, 1903.

Blessed Archie:

I think it was very cunning for you and Quentin to write me that letter together. I wish you could have been with me today on Algonquin, for we had a perfectly lovely ride. Dr. Rixey and I were on two very handsome horses, with Mexican saddles and bridles; the reins of very slender leather with silver rings. The road led through pine and cypress forests and along the beach. The surf was beating on the rocks in one place and right between two of the rocks where I really did not see how anything could swim a seal appeared and stood up on his tail half out of the foaming water and flapped his flippers, and was as much at home as anything could be. Beautiful gulls flew close to us all around, and cormorants swam along the breakers or walked along the beach.

I have a number of treasures to divide among you children when I get back. One of the treasures is Bill the Lizard. He is a little live lizard, called a horned frog, very cunning, who lives in a small box. The little badger, Josh, is very well and eats milk and potatoes. We took him out and gave him a run in the sand today. So far he seems as friendly as possible. When he feels hungry he squeals and the colored porters insist that he says "Du-la-ny, Du-la-ny," because Dulany is very good to him and takes care of him.

"Don't Play in the Library"
White House, June 12th, 1904.

Blessed Archie-kins:

Give my love to Mademoiselle; I hope you and Quenty are very good with her—and don't play in the library!

I loved your letter, and think you were good to write.

All kinds of live things are sent me from time to time. The other day an eagle came; this morning an owl.

(I have drawn him holding a rat in one claw.)

We sent both to the Zoo.

The other day while walking with Mr. Pinchot and Mr. Garfield we climbed into the Blagden deer park and almost walked over such a pretty wee fawn, all spotted; it ran off like a little race horse.

MORE ON BILL THE LIZARD
White House, June 21, 1904.

Blessed Archikins:

The other day when Mother and I were walking down the steps of the big south porch we saw a movement among the honeysuckles and there was Bill the lizard—your lizard that you brought home from Mount Vernon. We have seen him several times since and he is evidently entirely at home here. The White House seems big and empty without any of you children puttering around it, and I think the ushers miss you very much. I play tennis in the late afternoons unless I go to ride with Mother.

OUR LONELY DOG
White House, April 1, 1906.

Darling Archie:

Poor Skip is a very, very lonely little dog without his family. Each morning he comes up to see me at breakfast time and during most of breakfast (which I take in the hall just outside my room) Skip stands with his little paws on my lap. Then when I get through and sit down in the rocking-chair to read for fifteen or twenty minutes, Skip hops into my lap and stays there, just bathing himself in the companionship of the only one of his family he has left. The rest of the day he spends with the ushers, as I am so frightfully busy that I am nowhere long enough for Skip to have any real satisfaction in my companionship. Poor Jack has never come home. We may never know what became of him.

Mourning Skip
Sagamore Hill, Sept. 21, 1907.

Blessed Archiekins:

We felt dreadfully homesick as you and Kermit drove away; when we pass along the bay front we always think of the dory; and we mourn dear little Skip, although perhaps it was as well the little doggie should pass painlessly away, after his happy little life; for the little fellow would have pined for you.

Your letter was a great comfort; we'll send on the football suit and hope you'll enjoy the football. Of course it will all be new and rather hard at first.

The house is "put up;" everything wrapped in white that can be, and all the rugs off the floors. Quentin is reduced to the secret service men for steady companionship.

Quentin's King Snake
White House, Sept. 28, 1907.

Dearest Archie:

Before we left Oyster Bay Quentin had collected two snakes. He lost one, which did not turn up again until an hour before departure, when he found it in one of the spare rooms. This one he left loose, and brought the other one to Washington, there being a variety of exciting adventures on the way; the snake wriggling out of his box once, and being upset on the floor once. The first day home Quentin was allowed not to go to school but to go about and renew all his friendships. Among other places that he visited was Schmid's animal store, where he left his little snake. Schmid presented him with three snakes, simply to pass the day with-a large and beautiful and very friendly king snake and two little wee snakes. Quentin came hurrying back on his roller skates and burst into the room to show me his treasures. I was discussing certain matters with the Attorney-General at the time, and the snakes were eagerly deposited in my lap. The king snake, by the way, although most friendly with Quentin, had just been making a resolute effort to devour one of the smaller snakes. As Quentin and his menagerie were an interruption to my interview with the Department of Justice, I suggested that he go into the next room, where four Congressmen were drearily waiting until I should be at leisure. I thought that he and his snakes would probably enliven their waiting time. He at once fell in with the suggestion and rushed up to the Congressmen with the assurance that he would there find kindred spirits. They at first thought the snakes were wooden ones, and there was some perceptible recoil when they realized that they were alive. Then the king snake went up Quentin's sleeve—he was three or four feet long—and we hesitated to drag him back because his scales rendered that difficult. The last I saw of Quentin, one Congressman was gingerly helping him off with his jacket, so as to let the snake crawl out of the upper end of the sleeve.

LAST PRESIDENTIAL TRIP
On Board U. S. S. Mississippi, Oct. 1, 1907.

Dear Archie:

I am now on what I believe will be my last trip of any consequence while I am President. Until I got to Keokuk, Iowa, it was about like any other trip, but it is now pleasant going down the Mississippi, though I admit that I would rather be at home. We are on a funny, stern-wheel steamer. Mr. John McIlhenny is with me, and Capt. Seth Bullock among others. We have seen wild geese and ducks and cormorants on the river, and the people everywhere come out in boats and throng or cluster on the banks to greet us.

October 4

You would be greatly amused at these steamboats, and I think you will like your trip up the Mississippi next spring, if only everything goes right, and Mother is able to make it. There is no hold to the boat, just a flat bottom with a deck, and on this deck a foot or so above the water stands the engine-room, completely open at the sides and all the machinery visible as you come up to the boat. Both ends are blunt, and the gangways are drawn up to big cranes. Of course the boats could not stand any kind of a sea, but here they are very useful, for they are shallow and do not get hurt when they bump into the bank or one another. The river runs down in a broad, swirling, brown current, and nobody but an expert could tell the channel. One pilot or another is up in the Texas all day long and all night. Now the channel goes close under one bank, then we have to cross the river and go under the other bank; then there will come a deep spot when we can go anywhere. Then we wind in and out among shoals and sand-bars. At night the steamers are all lighted up, for there are a dozen of them in company with us. It is nice to look back at them as they twist after us in a long winding line down the river.

NAMES OF THE GUNS

On Board U. S. S. Louisiana,
Sunday, November 11, 1906.

Blessed Archie:

I wish you were along with us, for you would thoroughly enjoy everything on this ship. We have had three days of perfect weather, while this great battleship with her two convoys, the great armored cruisers, Tennessee and Washington, have steamed steadily in column ahead southward through calm seas until now we are in the tropics. They are three as splendid ships of their class as there are afloat, save only the English Dreadnaught. The Louisiana now has her gun-sights and everything is all in good shape for her to begin the practice of the duties which will make her crew as fit for man-of-war's work as the crew of any one of our other first-class battleships. The men are such splendid-looking fellows, Americans of the best type, young, active, vigorous, with lots of intelligence. I was much amused at the names of the seven-inch guns, which include

Victor, Invincible, Peacemaker, together with Skidoo, and also one called Tedd and one called The Big Stick.

A BUSY DAD LONGS FOR HIS SONS
White House, Jan. 2, 1908.

Dear Archie:

Friday night Quentin had three friends, including the little Taft boy, to spend the night with him. They passed an evening and night of delirious rapture, it being a continuous rough-house save when they would fall asleep for an hour or two from sheer exhaustion. I interfered but once, and that was to stop an exquisite jest of Quentin's, which consisted in procuring sulphureted hydrogen to be used on the other boys when they got into bed. They played hard, and it made me realize how old I had grown and how very busy I had been these last few years, to find that they had grown so that I was not needed in the play. Do you recollect how we all of us used to play hide-and-go-seek in the White House? and have obstacle races down the hall when you brought in your friends?

Mother continues much attached to Scamp, who is certainly a cunning little dog. He is very affectionate, but so exceedingly busy when we are out on the grounds, that we only catch glimpses of him zigzagging at full speed from one end of the place to the other. The kitchen cat and he have strained relations but have not yet come to open hostility.

The Adventures of Scamp
White House, Jan. 27, 1908.

Dear Archie:

Scamp is really a cunning little dog, but he takes such an extremely keen interest in hunting, and is so active, that when he is out on the grounds with us we merely catch glimpses of him as he flashes by. The other night after the Judicial Reception when we went up-stairs to supper the kitchen cat suddenly appeared parading down the hall with great friendliness, and was forthwith exiled to her proper home again.

Taking After Dad
White House, March 8, 1908.

Dearest Archie:

Yesterday morning Quentin brought down all his Force School baseball nine to practice on the White House grounds. It was great fun to see them, and Quentin made a run. It reminded me of when you used to come down with the Friend's School eleven. Moreover, I was reminded of the occasional rows in the eleven by an outburst in connection with the nine which resulted in their putting off of it a small boy who Quentin assured me was the "meanest kid in town." I like to see Quentin practicing baseball. It gives me hopes that one of my boys will not take after his father in this respect, and will prove able to play the national game!

Ethel has a delightful new dog—a white bull terrier—not much more than a puppy as yet. She has named it Mike and it seems very affectionate. Scamp is really an extraordinary ratter, and kills a great many rats in the White House, in the cellars and on the lower floor and among the machinery. He is really a very nice little dog.

Responsibility With Animals
White House, March 15, 1908.

Dearest Archie:

Quentin is now taking a great interest in baseball. Yesterday the Force School nine, on which he plays second base, played the P Street nine on the White House grounds where Quentin has marked out a diamond. The Force School nine was victorious by a score of 22 to 5. I told Quentin I was afraid the P Street boys must have felt badly and he answered, "Oh, I guess not; you see I filled them up with lemonade afterward!"

Charlie Taft is on his nine.

Did you hear of the dreadful time Ethel had with her new bull terrier, Mike? She was out riding with Fitz Lee, who was on Roswell, and Mike was following. They suppose that Fidelity must have accidentally kicked Mike. The first they knew the bulldog sprang at the little mare's throat. She fought pluckily, rearing and plunging, and shook him off, and then Ethel galloped away. As soon as she halted, Mike overtook her and attacked Fidelity again. He seized her by the shoulder and tried to seize her by the throat, and twice Ethel had to break away and gallop off, Fitz Lee endeavoring in vain to catch the dog. Finally he succeeded, just as Mike had got Fidelity by the hock. He had to give Mike a tremendous beating to restore him to obedience; but of course Mike will have to be disposed of. Fidelity was bitten in several places and it was a wonder that Ethel was able to keep her seat, because naturally the frightened little mare reared and plunged and ran.

SPITBALLS IN THE WHITE HOUSE
White House, April 11, 1908.

Dearest Archie:

Ethel has bought on trial an eight-months bulldog pup. He is very cunning, very friendly, and wriggles all over in a frantic desire to be petted.

Quentin really seems to be getting on pretty well with his baseball. In each of the last two games he made a base hit and a run. I have just had to give him and three of his associates a dressing down—one of the three being Charlie Taft. Yesterday afternoon was rainy, and four of them played five hours inside the White House. They were very boisterous and were all the time on the verge of mischief, and finally they made spit-balls and deliberately put them on the portraits. I did not discover it until after dinner, and then pulled Quentin out of bed and had him take them all off the portraits, and this morning required him to bring in the three other culprits before me. I explained to them that they had acted like boors; that it would have been a disgrace to have behaved so in any gentleman's house; that Quentin could have no friend to see him, and the other three could not come inside the White House, until I felt that a sufficient time had elapsed to serve as punishment. They were four very sheepish small boys when I got through with them.

FLYING SQUIRRELS
White House, May 10, 1908.

Dearest Archie:

Mother and I had great fun at Pine Knot. Mr. Burroughs, whom I call Oom John, was with us and we greatly enjoyed having him. But one night he fell into great disgrace! The flying squirrels that were there last Christmas had raised a brood, having built a large nest inside of the room in which you used to sleep and in which John Burroughs slept. Of course they held high carnival at night-time. Mother and I do not mind them at all, and indeed rather like to hear them scrambling about, and then as a sequel to a sudden frantic fight between two of them, hearing or seeing one little fellow come plump down to the floor and scuttle off again to the wall. But one night they waked up John Burroughs and he spent a misguided hour hunting for the nest, and when he found it took it down and caught two of the young squirrels and put them in a basket. The next day under Mother's direction I took them out, getting my fingers somewhat bitten in the process, and loosed them in our room, where we had previously put back the nest. I do not think John Burroughs profited by his misconduct, because the squirrels were more active than ever that night both in his room and ours, the disturbance in their family affairs having evidently made them restless!

THE BLESSINGS OF SPRING
White House, May 17, 1908.

Dearest Archie:

Quentin is really doing pretty well with his baseball, and he is perfectly absorbed in it. He now occasionally makes a base hit if the opposing pitcher is very bad; and his nine wins more than one-half of its games.

The grounds are too lovely for anything, and spring is here, or rather early summer, in full force. Mother's flower-gardens are now as beautiful as possible, and the iron railings of the fences south of them are covered with clematis and roses in bloom. The trees are in full foliage and the grass brilliant green, and my friends, the warblers, are trooping to the north in full force.

KNEELING WHILE PRAYING
White House, May 30, 1908.

Dearest Archie:

Quentin has met with many adventures this week; in spite of the fact that he has had a bad cough which has tended to interrupt the variety of his career. He has become greatly interested in bees, and the other day started down to get a beehive from somewhere, being accompanied by a mongrel looking small boy as to whose name I inquired. When repeated by Quentin it was obviously an Italian name. I asked who he was and Quentin responded: "Oh, his father keeps a fruit-stand." However, they got their bees all right and Quentin took the hive up to a school exhibit. There some of the bees got out and were left behind ("Poor homeless miserables," as Quentin remarked of them), and yesterday they at intervals added great zest to life in the classroom. The hive now reposes in the garden and Scamp surveys it for hours at a time with absorbed interest. After a while he will get to investigating it, and then he will find out more than he expects to.

This afternoon Quentin was not allowed to play ball because of his cough, so he was keeping the score when a foul tip caught him in the eye. It was quite a bad blow, but Quentin was very plucky about it and declined to go in until the game was finished, an hour or so later. By that time his eye had completely shut up and he now has a most magnificent bandage around his head over that eye, and feels much like a baseball hero. I came in after dinner to take a look at him and to my immense amusement found that he was lying flat on his back in bed saying his prayers, while Mademoiselle was kneeling down. It took me a moment or two to grasp the fact that good Mademoiselle wished to impress on him that it was not right to say his prayers unless he knelt down, and as that in this case he could not kneel down she would do it in his place!

The Last Hunt
Gondokoro, Feb. 27, 1910.

Dearest Archie:

Here, much to my pleasure, I find your letter written after the snow-storm at Sagamore. No snow here! On two or three days the thermometer at noon has stood at 115 degrees in the shade. All three naturalists and Mr. Cunninghame, the guide, have been sick, and so Kermit and I made our last hunt alone, going for eight days into the Lado. We were very successful, getting among other things three giant eland, which are great prizes. We worked hard; Kermit of course worked hardest, for he is really a first-class walker and runner; I had to go slowly, but I kept at it all day and every day. Kermit has really become not only an excellent hunter but also a responsible and trustworthy man, fit to lead; he managed the whole caravan and after hunting all day he would sit up half the night taking care of the skins. He is also the nicest possible companion. We are both very much attached to our gun-bearers and tent boys, and will be sorry to part with them.

A Scramble At Rock Creek Park
White House, Nov. 8, 1908.

Dearest Archie:

Quentin is getting along very well; he plays centre on his football eleven, and in a match for juniors in tennis he got into the semi-finals. What is more important, he seems to be doing very well with his studies, and to get on well with the boys, and is evidently beginning to like the school. He has shown himself very manly. Kermit is home now, and is a perfect dear.

The other day while taking a scramble walk over Rock Creek, when I came to that smooth-face of rock which we get round by holding on to the little bit of knob that we call the Button, the top of this button came off between my thumb and forefinger. I hadn't supposed that I was putting much weight on it, but evidently I was, for I promptly lost my balance, and finding I was falling, I sprang out into the creek. There were big rocks in it, and the water was rather shallow, but I landed all right and didn't hurt myself the least bit in the world.

A Steam Engine for Quentin
White House, Nov. 22, 1908.

Dearest Archie:

I handed your note and the two dollar bill to Quentin, and he was perfectly delighted. It came in very handy, because poor Quentin has been in bed with his leg in a plaster cast, and the two dollars I think went to make up a fund with which he purchased a fascinating little steam-engine, which has been a great source of amusement to him. He is out today visiting some friends, although his leg is still in a cast. He has a great turn for mechanics.

DOGS AND CATS
White House, Nov. 27, 1908.

Blessed Archie:

It is fine to hear from you and to know you are having a good time. Quentin, I am happy to say, is now thoroughly devoted to his school. He feels that he is a real Episcopal High School boy, and takes the keenest interest in everything. Yesterday, Thanksgiving Day, he had various friends here. His leg was out of plaster and there was nothing he did not do. He roller-skated; he practised football; he had engineering work and electrical work; he went all around the city; he romped all over the White House; he went to the slaughter-house and got a pig for Thanksgiving dinner.

Ethel is perfectly devoted to Ace, who adores her. The other day he was lost for a little while; he had gone off on a side street and unfortunately saw a cat in a stable and rushed in and killed it, and they had him tied up there when one of our men found him.

In a way I know that Mother misses Scamp, but in another way she does not, for now all the squirrels are very tame and cunning and are hopping about the lawn and down on the paths all the time, so that we see them whenever we walk, and they are not in the least afraid of us.

Triumph as a Rabbit Hunter
White House, Dec. 3, 1908.

Dearest Archie:

Quentin went out shooting with Dr. Rixey on Monday and killed three rabbits, which I think was pretty good. He came back very dirty and very triumphant, and Mother, feeling just as triumphant, brought him promptly over with his gun and his three rabbits to see me in the office. On most days now he rides out to school, usually on Achilles. Very shortly he will begin to spend his nights at the school, however. He has become sincerely attached to the school, and at the moment thinks he would rather stay there than go to Groton; but this is a thought he will get over-with Mother's active assistance. He has all kinds of friends, including some who are on a hockey team with him here in the city. The hockey team apparently plays hockey now and then, but only very occasionally, and spends most of the time disciplining its own members.

QUENTIN GROWN-UP
New York, Dec. 23, 1911.

Dear Archie:

Quentin turned up last night. He is half an inch taller than I am, and is in great shape. He is much less fat than he was, and seems to be turning out right in every way. I was amused to have him sit down and play the piano pretty well. We miss you dreadfully now that Christmas has come. The family went into revolt about my slouch hat, which Quentin christened "Old Mizzoura," and so I have had to buy another with a less pronounced crown and brim. We all drank your good health at dinner.

LETTERS TO
QUENTIN

Teddy Models Love of Creation
White House, June 12th, 1904.

Blessed Quenty-quee:

The little birds in the nest in the vines on the garden fence are nearly grown up. Their mother still feeds them.

You see the mother bird with a worm in her beak, and the little birds with their beaks wide open!

I was out walking the other day and passed the Zoo; there I fed with grass some of the two-year-old elk; the bucks had their horns "in the velvet." I fed them through the bars.

It made great jumps and held its white tail straight in the air.

Teddy Roosevelt and Uncle Remus
White House, June 21, 1904.

Dear Quentyquee:

The other day when out riding what should I see in the road ahead of me but a real B'rer Terrapin and B'rer Rabbit. They were sitting solemnly beside one another and looked just as if they had come out of a book; but as my horse walked along B'rer Rabbit went lippity lippity lippity off into the bushes and B'rer Terrapin drew in his head and legs till I passed.

MISSING AND LOVING YOU
White House, April 1, 1906.

Darling Quenty-quee:

Slipper and the kittens are doing finely. I think the kittens will be big enough for you to pet and have some satisfaction out of when you get home, although they will be pretty young still. I miss you all dreadfully, and the house feels big and lonely and full of echoes with nobody but me in it; and I do not hear any small scamps running up and down the hall just as hard as they can; or hear their voices while I am dressing; or suddenly look out through the windows of the office at the tennis ground and see them racing over it or playing in the sand-box. I love you very much.

COON CLAMOR ABOARD SHIP
On Board U. S. S. Louisiana, On the Way to Panama. Sunday, November 11, 1906.

Blessed Quentin:

You would be amused at the pets they have aboard this ship. They have two young bull-dogs, a cat, three little raccoons, and a tiny Cuban goat. They seem to be very amicable with one another, although I think the cat has suspicions of all the rest. The coons clamber about everywhere, and the other afternoon while I was sitting reading, I suddenly felt my finger seized in a pair of soft black paws and found the coon sniffing at it, making me feel a little uncomfortable

lest it might think the finger something good to eat. The
two puppies play endlessly. One of them belongs to
Lieutenant Evans. The crew will not be allowed ashore at
Panama or else I know they would pick up a whole raft of
other pets there. The jackies seem especially fond of the
little coons. A few minutes ago I saw one of the jackies
strolling about with a coon perched upon his shoulder, and
now and then he would reach up his hand and give it a small
piece of bread to eat.

LETTERS ABOUT
HIS CHILDREN

TEDDY'S OBSERVATIONS ON HIS BOY BIBLE COMMENTATORS

Oyster Bay, Dec. 8, 1900.

To Miss Emily T. Carow:

The other day I listened to a most amusing dialogue at the Bible lesson between Kermit and Ethel. The subject was Joseph, and just before reading it they had been reading Quentin's book containing the adventures of the Gollywogs. Joseph's conduct in repeating his dream to his brothers, whom it was certain to irritate, had struck both of the children unfavorably, as conflicting both with the laws of common-sense and with the advice given them by their parents as to the proper method of dealing with their own brothers and sisters. Kermit said: "Well, I think that was very foolish of Joseph." Ethel chimed in with "So do I, very foolish, and I do not understand how he could have done it." Then, after a pause, Kermit added thoughtfully by way of explanation: "Well, I guess he was simple, like Jane in the Gollywogs;" and Ethel nodded gravely in confirmation.

It is very cunning to see Kermit and Archie go to the Cove school together. They also come down and chop with me, Archie being armed with a hatchet blunt enough to be suitable for his six years. He is a most industrious small chopper, and the other day gnawed down, or as the children call it, "beavered" down, a misshapen tulip tree, which was about fifty feet high.

CALVINISTIC GUINEA PIGS
Oyster Bay, Nov. 22, 1900.

To E. S. Martin:

Mrs. Roosevelt and I were more touched than I can well say at your sending us your book with its characteristic insertion and above all with the little extract from your boy's note about Ted. In what Form is your boy? As you have laid yourself open, I shall tell you that Ted sings in the choir and is captain of his dormitory football team. He was awfully homesick at first, but now he has won his place in his own little world and he is all right. In his last letter to his mother in response to a question about his clothes he answered that they were in good condition, excepting "that one pair of pants was split up the middle and one jacket had lost a sleeve in a scuffle, and in another pair of pants he had sat down in a jam pie at a cellar spread." We have both missed him greatly in spite of the fact that we have five remaining. Did I ever tell you about my second small boy's names for his Guinea pigs? They included Bishop Doane; Dr. Johnson, my Dutch Reformed pastor; Father G. Grady, the local priest with whom the children had scraped a speaking acquaintance; Fighting Bob Evans, and Admiral Dewey. Some of my Republican supporters in West Virginia have just sent me a small bear which the children of their own accord christened Jonathan Edwards, partly out of compliment to their mother's ancestor, and partly because they thought they detected Calvinistic traits in the bear's character.

QUENTIN AND TURNER
Oyster Bay, June 29, 1908.

To Mrs. Nicholas Longworth,
Cincinnati, Ohio:

Quentin is really too funny for anything. He got his legs fearfully sunburned the other day, and they blistered, became inflamed, and ever-faithful Mother had to hold a clinic on him. Eyeing his blistered and scarlet legs, he remarked, "They look like a Turner sunset, don't they?" And then, after a pause, "I won't be caught again this way! quoth the raven, 'Nevermore!'" I was not surprised at his quoting Poe, but I would like to know where the ten-year-old scamp picked up any knowledge of Turner's sunsets.

LOVES AND SPORTS OF THE CHILDREN
Oyster Bay, Aug. 6, 1903.

To Miss Emily T. Carow:

To-day is Edith's birthday, and the children have been too cunning in celebrating it. Ethel had hemstitched a little handkerchief herself, and she had taken her gift and the gifts of all the other children into her room and neatly wrapped them up in white paper and tied with ribbons. They were for the most part taken down-stairs and put at her plate at breakfast time. Then at lunch in marched Kermit and Ethel with a cake, burning forty-two candles, and each candle with a piece of paper tied to it purporting to show the animal or inanimate object from which the candle came. All the dogs and horses—Renown, Bleistein, Yagenka, Algonquin, Sailor Boy, Brier, Hector, etc., as well as Tom Quartz, the cat, the extraordinarily named hens— such as Baron Speckle and Fierce, and finally even the boats and that pomegranate which Edith gave Kermit and which has always been known as Santiago, had each his or her or its tag on a special candle.

Edith is very well this summer and looks so young and pretty. She rides with us a great deal and loves Yagenka as much as ever. We also go out rowing together, taking our lunch and a book or two with us. The children fairly worship her, as they ought to, for a more devoted mother never was known. The children themselves are as cunning and good as possible. Ted is nearly as tall as I am and as tough and wiry as you can imagine. He is a really good rider and can hold his own in walking, running, swimming, shooting, wrestling, and boxing. Kermit is as cunning as ever and has developed greatly. He and his inseparable Philip started out for a night's camping in their best the other day. A driving storm came up and they had to put back, really showing both pluck, skill and judgment. They reached home, after having been out twelve hours, at nine in the evening. Archie continues devoted to Algonquin and to Nicholas. Ted's playmates are George and Jack, Aleck Russell, who is in Princeton, and Ensign Hamner of the Sylph. They wrestle, shoot, swim, play tennis, and go off on long expeditions in the boats. Quenty-quee has cast off the trammels of the nursery and become a most active and fearless though very good-tempered little boy. Really the children do have an ideal time out here, and it is an ideal place for them. The three sets of cousins are always together. I am rather disconcerted by the fact that they persist in regarding me as a playmate. This afternoon, for instance, was rainy, and all of them from George, Ted, Lorraine and Ethel down to Archibald, Nicholas and Quentin, with the addition of Aleck Russell and Ensign Hamner, came to get me to play with them in the old barn. They plead so hard that I finally gave in, but upon my word, I hardly knew whether it was quite right for the President to be engaged in such wild romping as the next two hours saw. The barn is filled with hay, and of course meets every requirement for the most active species of hide-and-seek and the like. Quentin enjoyed the game as much as any one, and would jump down from one hay level to another fifteen feet below with complete abandon.

I took Kermit and Archie, with Philip, Oliver, and Nicholas out for a night's camping in the two rowboats last week. They enjoyed themselves heartily, as usual, each sleeping rolled up in his blanket, and all getting up at an unearthly hour. Also, as usual, they displayed a touching and firm conviction that my cooking is unequalled. It was of a simple character, consisting of frying beefsteak first and then potatoes in bacon fat, over the camp fire; but they certainly ate in a way that showed their words were not uttered in a spirit of empty compliment.

THE ART OF UNCLE REMUS
White House, Oct. 12, 1901.

To Joel Chandler Harris:

It is worth while being President when one's small daughter receives that kind of an autograph gift. When I was younger than she is, my Aunt Annie Bulloch, of Georgia, used to tell me some of the brer rabbit stories, especially brer rabbit and the tar baby. But fond though I am of the brer rabbit stories I think I am even fonder of your other writings. I doubt if there is a more genuinely pathetic tale in all our literature than "Free Joe." Moreover I have felt that all that you write serves to bring our people closer together. I know, of course, the ordinary talk is that an artist should be judged purely by his art; but I am rather a Philistine and like to feel that the art serves a good purpose. Your art is not only an art addition to our sum of national achievement, but it has also always been an addition to the forces that tell for decency, and above all for the blotting out of sectional antagonism.

A PRESIDENT AT PLAY
Oyster Bay, Aug. 16, 1903.

To Miss Emily T. Carow:

Archie and Nick continue inseparable. I wish you could have seen them the other day, after one of the picnics, walking solemnly up, jointly carrying a basket, and each with a captured turtle in his disengaged hand. Archie is a most warm-hearted, loving, cunning little goose. Quentin, a merry soul, has now become entirely one of the children, and joins heartily in all their plays, including the romps in the old barn. When Ethel had her birthday, the one entertainment for which she stipulated was that I should take part in and supervise a romp in the old barn, to which all the Roosevelt children, Ensign Hamner of the Sylph, Bob Ferguson and Aleck Russell were to come. Of course I had not the heart to refuse; but really it seems, to put it mildly, rather odd for a stout, elderly President to be bouncing over hay-ricks in a wild effort to get to goal before an active midget of a competitor, aged nine years. However, it was really great fun.

One of our recent picnics was an innovation, due to Edith. We went in carriages or on horseback to Jane's Hill, some eight miles distant. The view was lovely, and there was a delightful old farmhouse half a mile away, where we left our horses. Speck (German Ambassador, Count Speck von Sternberg) rode with Edith and me, looking more like Hans Christian Andersen's little tin soldier than ever. His papers as Ambassador had finally come, and so he had turned up at Oyster Bay, together with the Acting Secretary of State, to present them. He appeared in what was really a very striking costume, that of a hussar. As soon as the ceremony was over, I told him to put on civilized raiment, which he did, and he spent a couple of days with me. We chopped, and shot, and rode together. He was delighted with Wyoming, and, as always, was extremely nice to the children.

The other day all the children gave amusing amateur theatricals, gotten up by Lorraine and Ted. The acting was upon Laura Roosevelt's tennis court. All the children were most cunning, especially Quentin as Cupid, in the scantiest of pink muslin tights and bodice. Ted and Lorraine, who were respectively George Washington and Cleopatra, really carried off the play. At the end all the cast joined hands in a song and dance, the final verse being devoted especially to me. I love all these children and have great fun with them, and I am touched by the way in which they feel that I am their special friend, champion, and companion.

To-day all, young and old, from the three houses went with us to Service on the great battleship Kearsarge—for the fleet is here to be inspected by me to-morrow. It was an impressive sight, one which I think the children will not soon forget. Most of the boys afterward went to lunch with the wretched Secretary Moody on the Dolphin. Ted had the younger ones very much on his mind, and when he got back said they had been altogether too much like a March Hare tea-party, as Archie, Nicholas and Oliver were not alive to the dignity of the occasion.

Prairie Girls
Divide Creek, Colo., April 26, 1905.

Darling Ethel:

Of course you remember the story of the little prairie girl. I always associate it with you. Well, again and again on this trip we would pass through prairie villages—bleak and lonely—with all the people in from miles about to see me. Among them were often dozens of young girls, often pretty, and as far as I could see much more happy than the heroine of the story. One of them shook hands with me, and then, after much whispering, said: "We want to shake hands with the guard!" The "guard" proved to be Roly, who was very swell in his uniform, and whom they evidently thought much more attractive than the President, both in age and looks.

There are plenty of ranchmen round here; they drive over to camp to see me, usually bringing a cake, or some milk and eggs, and are very nice and friendly. About twenty of the men came out with me, "to see the President shoot a bear"; and fortunately I did so in the course of an exhausting twelve hours' ride. I am very homesick for you all.

PRESIDENTIAL RESCUE OF A KITTEN
White House, June 24, 1906.

Darling Ethel:

To-day as I was marching to church, with Sloane some 25 yards behind, I suddenly saw two terriers racing to attack a kitten which was walking down the sidewalk. I bounced forward with my umbrella, and after some active work put to flight the dogs while Sloane captured the kitten, which was a friendly, helpless little thing, evidently too well accustomed to being taken care of to know how to shift for itself. I inquired of all the bystanders and of people on the neighboring porches to know if they knew who owned it; but as they all disclaimed, with many grins, any knowledge of it, I marched ahead with it in my arms for about half a block. Then I saw a very nice colored woman and little colored girl looking out of the window of a small house with on the door a dressmaker's advertisement, and I turned and walked up the steps and asked if they did not want the kitten. They said they did, and the little girl welcomed it lovingly; so I felt I had gotten it a home and continued toward church.

Has the lordly Ted turned up yet? Is his loving sister able, unassisted, to reduce the size of his head, or does she need any assistance from her male parent?

LONGING FOR HOME
Campalla, Dec. 23, 1909.

Blessedest Ethely-bye:

Here we are, the most wise Bavian—particularly nice—and the Elderly Parent, on the last stage of their journey. I am enjoying it all, but I think Kermit regards me as a little soft, because I am so eagerly looking forward to the end, when I shall see darling, pretty Mother, my own sweetheart, and the very nicest of all nice daughters—you blessed girlie. Do you remember when you explained, with some asperity, that of course you wished Ted were at home, because you didn't have anybody as a really intimate companion, whereas Mother had "old Father?" It is a great comfort to have a daughter to whom I can write about all kinds of intimate things!

This is a most interesting place. We crossed the great Nyanza Lake, in a comfortable steamer, in 24 hours, seeing a lovely sunset across the vast expanse of waters; and the moonlight later was as lovely. Here it is as hot as one would expect directly on the Equator, and the brilliant green landscape is fairly painted with even more brilliant flowers, on trees, bush, and vines; while the strange, semi-civilized people are most interesting. The queer little king's Prime Minister, an exceedingly competent, gorgeously dressed, black man, reminds Kermit of a rather civilized Umslopagaar—if that is the way you spell Rider Haggard's Zulu hero.

In this little native town we are driven round in rickshaws, each with four men pushing and pulling, who utter a queer, clanging note of exclamation in chorus, every few seconds, hour after hour.

Tribute to Kermit
On the 'Nzor River, Nov. 13, 1909.

Darling Ethel:

Here we are, by a real tropical river, with game all around, and no human being within several days' journey. At night the hyenas come round the camp, uttering their queer howls; and once or twice we have heard lions; but unfortunately have never seen them. Kermit killed a leopard yesterday. He has really done so very well! It is rare for a boy with his refined tastes and his genuine appreciation of literature—and of so much else—to be also an exceptionally bold and hardy sportsman. He is still altogether too reckless; but by my hen-with-one-chicken attitude, I think I shall get him out of Africa uninjured; and his keenness, cool nerve, horsemanship, hardihood, endurance, and good eyesight make him a really good wilderness hunter. We have become genuinely attached to Cunninghame and Tarleton, and all three naturalists, especially Heller; and also to our funny black attendants. The porters always amuse us; at this moment about thirty of them are bringing in the wood for the camp fires, which burn all night; and they are all chanting in chorus, the chant being nothing but the words "Wood-plenty of wood to burn!"

A Merry Christmas to you! And to Archie and Quentin. How I wish I were to be with you all, no matter how cold it might be at Sagamore; but I suppose we shall be sweltering under mosquito nets in Uganda.

PART II:
THE EARLY LIFE OF TEDDY ROOSEVELT

Love of peace is common among weak, short-sighted, timid, and lazy persons; and on the other hand courage is found among many men of evil temper and bad character. Neither quality shall by itself avail. Justice among the nations of mankind, and the uplifting of humanity, can be brought about only by those strong and daring men who with wisdom love peace, but who love righteousness more than peace.

—Teddy Roosevelt

Boyhood and Youth

*The following chapter was originally published in 1913 as part of
the book,* Theodore Roosevelt: An Autobiography. *In this
chapter, Roosevelt offers the reader an insight into the generational
legacy which contributed to the formation of one of the most vital
and outspoken men ever to sit in the White House.*—D.W.P.

Naturally grandfather on my father's side was of almost
purely Dutch blood. When he was young he still spoke some
Dutch, and Dutch was last used in the services of the Dutch
Reformed Church in New York while he was a small boy.

About 1644 his ancestor Klaes Martensen van
Roosevelt came to New Amsterdam as a "settler"—the
euphemistic name for an immigrant who came over in the
steerage of a sailing ship in the seventeenth century instead
of the steerage of a steamer in the nineteenth century. From
that time for the next seven generations from father to son
every one of us was born on Manhattan Island.

My father's paternal ancestors were of Holland stock;

except that there was one named Waldron, a wheelwright, who was one of the Pilgrims who remained in Holland when the others came over to found Massachusetts, and who then accompanied the Dutch adventurers to New Amsterdam. My father's mother was a Pennsylvanian. Her forbears had come to Pennsylvania with William Penn, some in the same ship with him; they were of the usual type of the immigration of that particular place and time. They included Welsh and English Quakers, an Irishman,—with a Celtic name, and apparently not a Quaker,—and peace-loving Germans, who were among the founders of Germantown, having been driven from their Rhineland homes when the armies of Louis the Fourteenth ravaged the Palatinate; and, in addition, representatives of a by-no-means altogether peaceful people, the Scotch-Irish, who came to Pennsylvania a little later, early in the eighteenth century. My grandmother was a woman of singular sweetness and strength, the keystone of the arch in her relations with her husband and sons. Although she was not herself Dutch, it was she who taught me the only Dutch I ever knew, a baby song of which the first line ran, "Trippe troppa tronjes." I always remembered this, and when I was in East Africa it proved a bond of union between me and the Boer settlers, not a few of whom knew it, although at first they always had difficulty in understanding my pronunciation—at which I do not wonder. It was interesting to meet these men whose ancestors had gone to the Cape about the time that mine went to America two centuries and a half previously, and to find that the descendants of the two streams of emigrants still crooned to their children some at least of the same nursery songs.

Of my great-grandfather Roosevelt and his family life a century and over ago I know little beyond what is implied in some of his books that have come down to me-the Letters of Junius, a biography of John Paul Jones, Chief Justice Marshall's "Life of Washington." They seem to indicate that his library was less interesting than that of my wife's great-grandfather at the same time, which certainly included such volumes as the original Edinburgh Review, for we have then now on our own book-shelves. Of my grandfather Roosevelt my most vivid childish reminiscence is not something I saw, but a tale that was told me concerning him. In his boyhood Sunday was as dismal a day for small Calvinistic children of Dutch descent as if they had been of Puritan or Scotch Covenanting or French Huguenot descent—and I speak as one proud of his Holland, Huguenot, and Covenanting ancestors, and proud that the blood of that stark Puritan divine Jonathan Edwards flows in the veins of his children. One summer afternoon, after listening to an unusually long Dutch Reformed sermon for the second time that day, my grandfather, a small boy, running home before the congregation had dispersed, ran into a party of pigs, which then wandered free in New York's streets. He promptly mounted a big boar, which no less promptly bolted and carried him at full speed through the midst of the outraged congregation.

By the way, one of the Roosevelt documents which came down to me illustrates the change that has come over certain aspects of public life since the time which pessimists term "the earlier and better days of the Republic." Old Isaac Roosevelt was a member of an Auditing Committee which shortly after the close of the Revolution approved the following bill:

The State of New York, to John Cape Dr.

To a Dinner Given by His Excellency the Governor and Council to their Excellencies the Minister of France and General Washington & Co.

1783 December

To	120 dinners at 48: 0:0
To	135 Bottles Madira 54: 0:0
"	36 ditto Port........................10:16:0
"	60 ditto English Beer............9: 0:0
"	30 Bouls Punch 9: 0:0
"	8 dinners for Musick...........1:12:0
"	10 ditto for Sarvts 2: 0:0
"	60 Wine Glasses Broken......4:10:0
"	8 Cutt decanters Broken 3: 0:0
"	Coffee for 8 Gentlemen 1:12:0
"	Music fees &ca.....................8: 0:0
"	Fruit & Nuts.........................5: 0:0

&sterling; 156:10:0

By Cash   100:16:0

55:14:0

We a Committee of Council having examined the above account do certify it (amounting to one hundred and fifty-six Pounds ten Shillings) to be just. December 17th 1783.

ISAAC ROOSEVELTT
JAS. DUANE
EGBT. BENSON
FRED. JAY

Received the above Contents in full New York 17th December 1783 John Cape.

Think of the Governor of New York now submitting such a bill for such an entertainment of the French

Ambassador and the President of the United States! Falstaff's views of the proper proportion between sack and bread are borne out by the proportion between the number of bowls of punch and bottles of port, Madeira, and beer consumed, and the "coffee for eight gentlemen"-apparently the only ones who lasted through to that stage of the dinner. Especially admirable is the nonchalant manner in which, obviously as a result of the drinking of said bottles of wine and bowls of punch, it is recorded that eight cut-glass decanters and sixty wine-glasses were broken.

During the Revolution some of my forefathers, North and South, served respectably, but without distinction, in the army, and others rendered similar service in the Continental Congress or in various local legislatures. By that time those who dwelt in the North were for the most part merchants, and those who dwelt in the South, planters.

My mother's people were predominantly of Scotch, but also of Huguenot and English, descent. She was a Georgian, her people having come to Georgia from South Carolina before the Revolution. The original Bulloch was a lad from near Glasgow, who came hither a couple of centuries ago, just as hundreds of thousands of needy, enterprising Scotchmen have gone to the four quarters of the globe in the intervening two hundred years. My mother's great-grandfather, Archibald Bulloch, was the first Revolutionary "President" of Georgia. My grandfather, her father, spent the winters in Savannah and the summers at Roswell, in the Georgia uplands near Atlanta, finally making Roswell his permanent home. He used to travel thither with his family and their belongings in his own carriage, followed by a baggage wagon. I never saw Roswell until I was President, but my mother told me so much about the place that when I did see it I felt as if I already knew every nook and corner of it, and as if it were haunted by the ghosts of all the men and women who had lived there. I do not mean merely my own family, I mean the slaves. My mother and her sister, my aunt, used to tell us children all kinds of stories about the slaves. One of the most fascinating referred to a very old darky called Bear Bob, because in the early days of settlement he had been partially scalped by a black bear. Then there was Mom' Grace, who was for a time my mother's nurse, and whom I had supposed to be dead, but who greeted me when I did come to Roswell, very respectable, and apparently with years of life before her. The two chief personages of the drama that used to be repeated to us were Daddy Luke, the Negro overseer, and his wife, Mom' Charlotte. I never saw either Daddy Luke or Mom' Charlotte, but I inherited the care of them when my mother died. After the close of the war they resolutely refused to be emancipated or leave the place. The only demand they made upon us was enough money annually to get a new "critter," that is, a mule. With a certain lack of ingenuity the mule was reported each Christmas as having passed away, or at least as having become so infirm as to necessitate a successor—a solemn fiction which neither deceived nor was intended to deceive, but which furnished a gauge for the size of the Christmas gift.

My maternal grandfather's house was on the line of Sherman's march to the sea, and pretty much everything in it that was portable was taken by the boys in blue, including most of the books in the library. When I was President the facts about my ancestry were published, and a former soldier in Sherman's army sent me back one of the books with my grandfather's name in it. It was a little copy of the poems of "Mr. Gray"—an eighteenth-century edition printed in Glasgow.

On October 27, 1858, I was born at No. 28 East Twentieth Street, New York City, in the house in which we lived during the time that my two sisters and my brother and I were small children. It was furnished in the canonical taste of the New York which George William Curtis described in the Potiphar Papers. The black haircloth furniture in the dining-room scratched the bare legs of the children when they sat on it. The middle room was a library, with tables, chairs, and bookcases of gloomy respectability. It was without windows, and so was available only at night. The front room, the parlor, seemed to us children to be a room of much splendor, but was open for general use only on Sunday evening or on rare occasions when there were parties. The Sunday evening family gathering was the redeeming feature in a day which otherwise we children did not enjoy—chiefly because we were all of us made to wear clean clothes and keep neat. The ornaments of that parlor I remember now, including the gas chandelier decorated with a great quantity of cut-glass prisms. These prisms struck me as possessing peculiar magnificence. One of them fell off one day, and I hastily grabbed it and stowed it away, passing several days of furtive delight in the treasure, a delight always alloyed with fear that I would be found out and convicted of larceny. There was a Swiss wood-carving representing a very big hunter on one side of an exceedingly small mountain, and a herd of chamois, disproportionately small for the hunter and large for the mountain, just across the ridge. This always fascinated us; but there was a small chamois kid for which we felt agonies lest the hunter might come on it and kill it. There was also a Russian moujik drawing a gilt sledge on a piece of malachite. Some one mentioned in my hearing that malachite was a valuable marble. This fixed in my mind that is was valuable exactly as diamonds are valuable. I accepted that moujik as a priceless work of art, and it was not until I was well in middle age that it occurred to me that I was mistaken.

Now and then we children were taken round to our grandfather's house; a big house for the New York of those days, on the corner of Fourteenth Street and Broadway, fronting Union Square. Inside there was a large hall running up to the roof; there was a tessellated black-and-white marble floor, and a circular staircase round the sides of the hall, from the top floor down. We children much admired both the tessellated floor and the circular staircase. I think we were right about the latter, but I am not so sure as to the tessellated floor.

The summers we spent in the country, now at one place, now at another. We children, of course, loved the country beyond anything. We disliked the city. We were always wildly eager to get to the country when spring came, and very sad when in the late fall the family moved back to town. In the country we of course had all kinds of pets—cats, dogs, rabbits, a coon, and a sorrel Shetland pony named General Grant. When my younger sister first heard of the real General Grant, by the way, she was much struck by the coincidence that some one should have given him the same name as the pony. (Thirty years later my own children had their pony Grant.) In the country we children ran barefoot much of the time, and the seasons went by in a round of uninterrupted and enthralling pleasures— supervising the haying and harvesting, picking apples, hunting frogs successfully and woodchucks unsuccessfully, gathering hickory-nuts and chestnuts for sale to patient parents, building wigwams in the woods, and sometimes playing Indians in too realistic manner by staining ourselves (and incidentally our clothes) in liberal fashion with poke-cherry juice. Thanksgiving was an appreciated festival, but it in no way came up to Christmas. Christmas was an occasion of literally delirious joy. In the evening we hung up our stockings—or rather the biggest stockings we could borrow from the grown-ups—and before dawn we trooped in to open them while sitting on father's and mother's bed; and the bigger presents were arranged, those for each child on its own table, in the drawing-room, the doors to which were thrown open after breakfast. I never knew any one else have what seemed to me such attractive Christmases, and in the next generation I tried to reproduce them exactly for my own children.

My father, Theodore Roosevelt, was the best man I ever knew. He combined strength and courage with gentleness, tenderness, and great unselfishness. He would not tolerate in us children selfishness or cruelty, idleness, cowardice, or untruthfulness. As we grew older he made us understand that the same standard of clean living was demanded for the boys as for the girls; that what was wrong in a woman could not be right in a man. With great love and patience, and the most understanding sympathy and consideration, he combined insistence on discipline. He never physically punished me but once, but he was the only man of whom I was ever really afraid. I do not mean that it was a wrong fear, for he was entirely just, and we children adored him. We used to wait in the library in the evening until we could hear his key rattling in the latch of the front hall, and then rush out to greet him; and we would troop into his room while he was dressing, to stay there as long as we were permitted, eagerly examining anything which came out of his pockets which could be regarded as an attractive novelty. Every child has fixed in his memory various details which strike it as of grave importance. The trinkets he used to keep in a little box on his dressing-table we children always used to speak of as "treasures." The word, and some of the trinkets themselves, passed on to the next generation. My own children, when small, used to troop into my room while I was dressing, and the gradually accumulating trinkets in the "ditty-box"—the gift of an enlisted man in the navy—always excited rapturous joy. On occasions of solemn festivity each child would receive a trinket for his or her "very own." My children, by the way, enjoyed one pleasure I do not remember enjoying myself. When I came back from riding, the child who brought the bootjack would itself promptly get into the boots, and clump up and down the room with a delightful feeling of kinship with Jack of the seven-league strides.

The punishing incident I have referred to happened

when I was four years old. I bit my elder sister's arm. I do not remember biting her arm, but I do remember running down to the yard, perfectly conscious that I had committed a crime. From the yard I went into the kitchen, got some dough from the cook, and crawled under the kitchen table. In a minute or two my father entered from the yard and asked where I was. The warm-hearted Irish cook had a characteristic contempt for "informers," but although she said nothing she compromised between informing and her conscience by casting a look under the table. My father immediately dropped on all fours and darted for me. I feebly heaved the dough at him, and, having the advantage of him because I could stand up under the table, got a fair start for the stairs, but was caught halfway up them. The punishment that ensued fitted the crime, and I hope—and believe—that it did me good.

I never knew any one who got greater joy out of living than did my father, or any one who more whole-heartedly performed every duty; and no one whom I have ever met approached his combination of enjoyment of life and performance of duty. He and my mother were given to a hospitality that at that time was associated more commonly with southern than northern households; and, especially in their later years when they had moved up town, in the neighborhood of Central Park, they kept a charming, open house.

My father worked hard at his business, for he died when he was forty-six, too early to have retired. He was interested in every social reform movement, and he did an immense amount of practical charitable work himself. He was a big, powerful man, with a leonine face, and his heart filled with gentleness for those who needed help or protection, and with the possibility of much wrath against a bully or an oppressor. He was very fond of riding both on the road and across the country, and was also a great whip. He usually drove four-in-hand, or else a spike team, that is, a pair with a third horse in the lead. I do not suppose that such a team exists now. The trap that he drove we always called the high phaëton. The wheels turned under in front. I have it yet. He drove long-tailed horses, harnessed loose in light American harness, so that the whole rig had no possible resemblance to anything that would be seen now. My father always excelled in improving every spare half-hour or three-quarters of an hour, whether for work or enjoyment. Much of his four-in-hand driving was done in the summer afternoons when he would come out on the trait from his business in New York.

My mother and one or perhaps two of us children might meet him at the station. I can see him now getting out of the car in his linen duster, jumping into the wagon, and instantly driving off at a rattling pace, the duster sometimes bagging like a balloon. The four-in-hand, as can be gathered from the above description, did not in any way in his eyes represent possible pageantry. He drove it because he liked it. He was always preaching caution to his boys, but in this respect he did not practice his preaching overmuch himself; and, being an excellent whip, he liked to take chances. Generally they came out all right. Occasionally they did not; but he was even better at getting out of a scrape than into it. Once when we were driving into

New York late at night the leaders stopped. He flicked them, and the next moment we could dimly make out that they had jumped. I then appeared that the street was closed and that a board had been placed across it, resting on two barrels, but without a lantern. Over this board the leaders had jumped, and there was considerable excitement before we got the board taken off the barrels and resumed our way. When in the city on Thanksgiving or Christmas, my father was very apt to drive my mother and a couple of friends up to the racing park to take lunch. But he was always back in time to go to the dinner at the Newsboys' Lodging-House, and not infrequently also to Miss Sattery's Night School for little Italians.

At a very early age we children were taken with him and were required to help. He was a staunch friend of Charles Loring Brace, and was particularly interested in the Newsboys' Lodging-House and in the night schools and in getting the children off the streets and out on farms in the West. When I was President, the Governor of Alaska under me, Governor Brady, was one of these ex-newsboys who had been sent from New York out West by Mr. Brace and my father. My father was greatly interested in the societies to prevent cruelty to children and cruelty to animals. On Sundays he had a mission class. On his way to it he used to drop us children at our Sunday-school in Dr. Adams's Presbyterian Church on Madison Square; I remember hearing my aunt, my mother's sister, saying that when he walked along with us children he always reminded her of Greatheart in Bunyan. Under the spur of his example I taught a mission class myself for three years before going to college and for all four years that I was in college. I do not think I made much of a success of it. But the other day on getting out of a taxi in New York the chauffeur spoke to me and told me that he was one of my old Sunday-school pupils. I remembered him well, and was much pleased to find that he was an ardent Bull Mooser!

My mother, Martha Bulloch, was a sweet, gracious, beautiful Southern woman, a delightful companion and beloved by everybody. She was entirely "unreconstructed" to the day of her death. Her mother, my grandmother, one of the dearest of old ladies, lived with us, and was distinctly overindulgent to us children, being quite unable to harden her heart towards us even when the occasion demanded it. Towards the close of the Civil War, although a very small boy, I grew to have a partial but alert understanding of the fact that the family were not one in their views about that conflict, my father being a strong Lincoln Republican; and once, when I felt that I had been wronged by maternal discipline during the day, I attempted a partial vengeance by praying with loud fervor for the success of the Union arms, when we all came to say our prayers before my mother in the evening. She was not only a most devoted mother, but was also blessed with a strong sense of humor, and she was too much amused to punish me; but I was warned not to repeat the offense, under penalty of my father's being informed—he being the dispenser of serious punishment. Morning prayers were with my father. We used to stand at the foot of the stairs, and when father came down we called out, "I speak for you and the cubby-hole too!" There were three of us young children, and we used to sit with father on the sofa while he conducted morning prayers. The place between father and the arm of the sofa we called the "cubby-hole." The child who got that place we regarded as especially favored both in comfort and somehow or other in rank and title. The two who were left to sit on the much wider expanse of sofa on the other side of father were outsiders for the time being.

My aunt Anna, my mother's sister, lived with us. She was as devoted to us children as was my mother herself, and we were equally devoted to her in return. She taught us our lessons while we were little. She and my mother used to entertain us by the hour with tales of life on the Georgia plantations; of hunting fox, deer, and wildcat; of the long-tailed driving horses, Boone and Crockett, and of the riding horses, one of which was named Buena Vista in a fit of patriotic exaltation during the Mexican War; and of the queer goings-on in the Negro quarters. She knew all the "Br'er Rabbit" stories, and I was brought up on them. One of my uncles, Robert Roosevelt, was much struck with them, and took them down from her dictation, publishing them in *Harper's*, where they fell flat. This was a good many years before a genius arose who in "Uncle Remus" made the stories immortal.

My mother's two brothers, James Dunwoodie Bulloch and Irvine Bulloch, came to visit us shortly after the close of the war. Both came under assumed names, as they were among the Confederates who were at that time exempted from the amnesty. "Uncle Jimmy" Bulloch was a dear old retired sea-captain, utterly unable to "get on" in the worldly sense of that phrase, as valiant and simple and upright a soul as ever lived, a veritable Colonel Newcome. He was an Admiral in the Confederate navy, and was the builder of the famous Confederate war vessel Alabama. My uncle Irvine Bulloch was a midshipman on the Alabama, and fired the last gun discharged from her batteries in the fight with the Kearsarge. Both of these uncles lived in Liverpool after the war.

My uncle Jimmy Bulloch was forgiving and just in reference to the Union forces, and could discuss all phases of the Civil War with entire fairness and generosity. But in English politics he promptly became a Tory of the most ultra-conservative school. Lincoln and Grant he could admire, but he would not listen to anything in favor of Mr. Gladstone. The only occasions on which I ever shook his faith in me were when I would venture meekly to suggest that some of the manifestly preposterous falsehoods about Mr. Gladstone could not be true. My uncle was one of the best men I have ever known, and when I have sometimes been tempted to wonder how good people can believe of me the unjust and impossible things they do believe, I have consoled myself by thinking of Uncle Jimmy Bulloch's perfectly sincere conviction that Gladstone was a man of quite exceptional and nameless infamy in both public and private life.

I was a sickly, delicate boy, suffered much from asthma, and frequently had to be taken away on trips to find a place where I could breathe. One of my memories is of my father walking up and down the room with me in his arms at night when I was a very small person, and of sitting up in bed gasping, with my father and mother trying to help me. I went very little to school. I never went to the public schools, as my own children later did, both at the "Cove School" at Oyster Bay and at the "Ford School" in Washington. For a few months I attended Professor McMullen's school in Twentieth Street near the house where I was born, but most of the time I had tutors. As I have already said, my aunt taught me when I was small. At one time we had a French governess, a loved and valued "mam'selle," in the household.

When I was ten years old I made my first journey to Europe. My birthday was spent in Cologne, and in order to give me a thoroughly "party" feeling I remember that my mother put on full dress for my birthday dinner. I do not think I gained anything from this particular trip abroad. I cordially hated it, as did my younger brother and sister. Practically all the enjoyment we had was in exploring any ruins or mountains when we could get away from our elders, and in playing in the different hotels. Our one desire was to get back to America, and we regarded Europe with the most ignorant chauvinism and contempt. Four years later, however, I made another journey to Europe, and was old enough to enjoy it thoroughly and profit by it.

While still a small boy I began to take an interest in natural history. I remember distinctly the first day that I started on my career as zoölogist. I was walking up Broadway, and as I passed the market to which I used sometimes to be sent before breakfast to get strawberries I suddenly saw a dead seal laid out on a slab of wood. That seal filled me with every possible feeling of romance and adventure. I asked where it was killed, and was informed in the harbor. I had already begun to read some of Mayne

Reid's books and other boys' books of adventure, and I felt that this seal brought all these adventures in realistic fashion before me. As long as that seal remained there I haunted the neighborhood of the market day after day. I measured it, and I recall that, not having a tape measure, I had to do my best to get its girth with a folding pocket foot-rule, a difficult undertaking. I carefully made a record of the utterly useless measurements, and at once began to write a natural history of my own, on the strength of that seal. This, and subsequent natural histories, were written down in blank books in simplified spelling, wholly unpremeditated and unscientific. I had vague aspirations of in some way or another owning and preserving that seal, but they never got beyond the purely formless stage. I think, however, I did get the seal's skull, and with two of my cousins promptly started what we ambitiously called the "Roosevelt Museum of Natural History." The collections were at first kept in my room, until a rebellion on the part of the chambermaid received the approval of the higher authorities of the household and the collection was moved up to a kind of bookcase in the back hall upstairs. It was the ordinary small boy's collection of curios, quite incongruous and entirely valueless except from the standpoint of the boy himself. My father and mother encouraged me warmly in this, as they always did in anything that could give me wholesome pleasure or help to develop me.

The adventure of the seal and the novels of Mayne Reid together strengthened my instinctive interest in natural history. I was too young to understand much of Mayne Reid, excepting the adventure part and the natural history part-these enthralled me. But of course my reading was not wholly confined to natural history. There was very little effort made to compel me to read books, my father and mother having the good sense not to try to get me to read anything I did not like, unless it was in the way of study. I was given the chance to read books that they thought I ought to read, but if I did not like them I was then given some other good book that I did like. There were certain books that were taboo. For instance, I was not allowed to read dime novels. I obtained some surreptitiously and did read them, but I do not think that the enjoyment compensated for the feeling of guilt. I was also forbidden to read the only one of Ouida's books which I wished to read—"Under Two Flags." I did read it, nevertheless, with greedy and fierce hope of coming on something unhealthy; but as a matter of fact all the parts that might have seemed unhealthy to an older person made no impression on me whatever. I simply enjoyed in a rather confused way the general adventures.

I think there ought to be children's books. I think that the child will like grown-up books also, and I do not believe a child's book is really good unless grown-ups get something out of it. For instance, there is a book I did not have when I was a child because it was not written. It is Laura E. Richard's "Nursery Rhymes." My own children loved them dearly, and their mother and I loved them almost equally; the delightfully light-hearted "Man from New Mexico who Lost his Grandmother out in the Snow," the adventures of "The Owl, the Eel, and the Warming-Pan," and the extraordinary genealogy of the kangaroo whose "father was a whale with a feather in his tail who lived in the Greenland sea," while "his mother was a shark who kept very dark in the Gulf of Caribee."

As a small boy I had Our Young Folks, which I then firmly believed to be the very best magazine in the world—a belief, I may add, which I have kept to this day unchanged, for I seriously doubt if any magazine for old or young has ever surpassed it. Both my wife and I have the bound volumes of Our Young Folks which we preserved from our youth. I have tried to read again the Mayne Reid books which I so dearly loved as a boy, only to find, alas! that it is impossible. But I really believe that I enjoy going over Our Young Folks now nearly as much as ever. "Cast Away in the Cold," "Grandfather's Struggle for a Homestead," "The William Henry Letters," and a dozen others like them were first-class, good healthy stories, interesting in the first place, and in the next place teaching manliness, decency, and good conduct. At the cost of being deemed effeminate, I will add that I greatly liked the girls' stories—"Pussy Willow" and "A Summer in Leslie Goldthwaite's Life," just as I worshiped "Little Men" and "Little Women" and "An Old-Fashioned Girl."

This enjoyment of the gentler side of life did not prevent my reveling in such tales of adventure as Ballantyne's stories, or Marryat's "Midshipman Easy." I suppose everybody has kinks in him, and even as a child there were books which I ought to have liked and did not. For instance, I never cared at all for the first part of "Robinson Crusoe" (and although it is unquestionably the best part, I do not care for it now); whereas the second part, containing the adventures of Robinson Crusoe, with the wolves in the Pyrenees, and out in the Far East, simply fascinated me. What I did like in the first part were the adventures before Crusoe finally reached his island, the fight with the Sallee Rover, and the allusion to the strange beasts at night taking their improbable bath in the ocean. Thanks to being already an embryo zoölogist, I dislike the "Swiss Family Robinson" because of the wholly impossible collection of animals met by that worthy family as they ambled inland from the wreck. Even in poetry it was the relation of adventures that most appealed to me as a boy. At a pretty early age I began to read certain books of poetry, notably Longfellow's poem, "The Saga of King Olaf," which absorbed me. This introduced me to Scandinavian literature; and I have never lost my interest in and affection for it.

Among my first books was a volume of a hopelessly unscientific kind by Mayne Reid, about mammals, illustrated with pictures no more artistic than but quite as thrilling as those in the typical school geography. When my father found how deeply interested I was in this not very accurate volume, he gave me a little book by J. G. Wood, the English writer of popular books on natural history, and then a larger one of his called "Homes Without Hands." Both of these were cherished possessions. They were studied eagerly; and they finally descended to my children. The "Homes Without Hands," by the way, grew to have an added association in connection with a pedagogical failure on my part. In accordance with what I believed was some kind of modern theory of making education interesting and not letting it become a task, I endeavored to teach my eldest small boy one or two of his letters from the title-page. As the letter "H" appeared in the title an unusual number of times, I selected that to begin on, my effort being to keep the small boy interested, not to let him realize that he was learning a lesson, and to convince him that he was merely having a good time. Whether it was the theory or my method of applying it that was defective I do not know, but I certainly absolutely eradicated from his brain any ability to learn what "H" was; and long after he had learned all the other letters of the alphabet in the old-fashioned way, he proved wholly unable to remember "H" under any circumstances.

Quite unknown to myself, I was, while a boy, under a hopeless disadvantage in studying nature. I was very near-sighted, so that the only things I could study were those I ran against or stumbled over. When I was about thirteen I was allowed to take lessons in taxidermy from a Mr. Bell, a tall, clean-shaven, white-haired old gentleman, as straight as an Indian, who had been a companion of Audubon's. He had a musty little shop, somewhat on the order of Mr. Venus's shop in "Our Mutual Friend," a little shop in which he had done very valuable work for science. This "vocational study," as I suppose it would be called by modern educators, spurred and directed my interest in collecting specimens for mounting and preservation. It was this summer that I got my first gun, and it puzzled me to find that my companions seemed to see things to shoot at which I could not see at all. One day they read aloud an advertisement in huge letters on a distant billboard, and I then realized that something was the matter, for not only was I unable to read the sign but I could not even see the letters. I spoke of this to my father, and soon afterwards got my first pair of spectacles, which literally opened an entirely new world to me. I had no idea how beautiful the world was until I got those spectacles. I had been a clumsy and awkward little boy, and while much of my clumsiness and awkwardness was doubtless due to general characteristics, a good deal of it was due to the fact that I could not see and yet was wholly ignorant that I was not seeing. The recollection of this experience gives me a keen sympathy with those who are trying in our public schools and elsewhere to remove the physical causes of deficiency in children, who are often unjustly blamed for being obstinate or unambitious, or mentally stupid.

This same summer, too, I obtained various new books on mammals and birds, including the publications of Spencer Baird, for instance, and made an industrious book-study of the subject. I did not accomplish much in outdoor study because I did not get spectacles until late in the fall, a short time before I started with the rest of the family for a second trip to Europe. We were living at Dobbs Ferry, on the Hudson. My gun was a breech-loading, pin-fire double-barrel, of French manufacture. It was an excellent gun for a clumsy and often absent-minded boy. There was no spring to open it, and if the mechanism became rusty it could be opened with a brick without serious damage. When the cartridges stuck they could be removed in the same fashion. If they were loaded, however, the result was not always happy, and I tattooed myself with partially unburned grains of powder more than once.

When I was fourteen years old, in the winter of '72 and '73, I visited Europe for the second time; and this trip formed a really useful part of my education. We went to Egypt, journeyed up the Nile, traveled through the Holy Land and part of Syria, visited Greece and Constantinople; and then we children spent the summer in a German family in Dresden. My first real collecting as a student of natural history was done in Egypt during this journey. By this time I had a good working knowledge of American bird life from the superficially scientific standpoint. I had no knowledge of the ornithology of Egypt, but I picked up in Cairo a book by an English clergyman, whose name I have now forgotten, who described a trip up the Nile, and in an appendix to his volume gave an account of his bird collection. I wish I could remember the name of the author now, for I owe that book very much. Without it I should have been collecting entirely in the dark, whereas with its aid I could generally find out what the birds were. My first knowledge of Latin was obtained by learning the scientific names of the birds and mammals which I collected and classified by the aid of such books as this one.

The birds I obtained up the Nile and in Palestine represented merely the usual boy's collection. Some years afterward I gave them, together with the other ornithological specimens I had gathered, to the Smithsonian Institution in Washington, and I think some of them also to the American Museum of Natural History in New York. I am told that the skins are to be found yet in both places and in other public collections. I doubt whether they have my original labels on them. With great pride the directors of the "Roosevelt Museum," consisting of myself and the two cousins aforesaid, had printed a set of Roosevelt Museum labels in pink ink preliminary to what was regarded as my adventurous trip to Egypt. This bird-collecting gave what was really the chief zest to my Nile journey. I was old enough and had read enough to enjoy the temples and the desert scenery and the general feeling of romance; but this in time would have palled if I had not also had the serious work of collecting and preparing my specimens. Doubtless the family had their moments of suffering—especially on one occasion when a well-meaning maid extracted from my taxidermist's outfit the old tooth-brush with which I put on the skins the arsenical soap necessary for their preservation, partially washed it, and left it with the rest of my wash kit for my own personal use. I suppose that all growing boys tend to be grubby; but the ornithological small boy, or indeed the boy with the taste for natural history of any kind, is generally the very grubbiest of all. An added element in my case was the fact that while in Egypt I suddenly started to grow. As there were no tailors up the Nile, when I got back to Cairo I needed a new outfit. But there was one suit of clothes too good to throw away, which we kept for a "change," and which was known as my "Smike suit," because it left my wrists and ankles as bare as those of poor Smike himself.

When we reached Dresden we younger children were left to spend the summer in the house of Herr Minckwitz, a member of either the Municipal or the Saxon Government—I have forgotten which. It was hoped that in this way we would acquire some knowledge of the German language and literature. They were the very kindest family imaginable. I shall never forget the unwearied patience of the two daughters. The father and mother, and a shy, thin, student cousin who was living in the flat, were no less kind. Whenever I could get out into the country I collected specimens industriously and enlivened the household with hedge-hogs and other small beasts and reptiles which persisted in escaping from partially closed bureau drawers. The two sons were fascinating students from the University of Leipsic, both of them belonging to dueling corps, and much scarred in consequence. One, a famous swordsman, was called Der Rothe Herzog (the Red Duke), and the other was nicknamed Herr Nasehorn (Sir Rhinoceros) because the tip of his nose had been cut off in a duel and sewn on again. I learned a good deal of German here, in spite of myself, and above all I became fascinated with the Nibelungenlied. German prose never became really easy to me in the sense that French prose did, but for German poetry I cared as much as for English poetry. Above all, I gained an impression of the German people which I never got over. From that time to this it would have been quite impossible to make me feel that the Germans were really foreigners. The affection, the Gemüthlichkeit (a quality which cannot be exactly expressed by any single English word), the capacity for hard work, the sense of duty, the delight in studying literature and science, the pride in the new Germany, the more than kind and friendly interest in three strange children-all these manifestations of the German character and of German family life made a subconscious impression upon me which I did not in the least define at the time, but which is very vivid still forty years later.

When I got back to America, at the age of fifteen, I began serious study to enter Harvard under Mr. Arthur Cutler, who later founded the Cutler School in New York. I could not go to school because I knew so much less than most boys of my age in some subjects and so much more in others. In science and history and geography and in unexpected parts of German and French I was strong, but lamentably weak in Latin and Greek and mathematics. My grandfather had made his summer home in Oyster Bay a number of years before, and my father now made Oyster Bay the summer home of his family also. Along with my college preparatory studies I carried on the work of a practical student of natural history. I worked with greater industry than either intelligence or success, and made very few additions to the sum of human knowledge; but to this day certain obscure ornithological publications may be found in which are recorded such items as, for instance, that on one occasion a fish-crow, and on another an Ipswich sparrow, were obtained by one Theodore Roosevelt, Jr., at Oyster Bay, on the shore of Long Island Sound.

In the fall of 1876 I entered Harvard, graduating in 1880. I thoroughly enjoyed Harvard, and I am sure it did me good, but only in the general effect, for there was very little in my actual studies which helped me in after life. More than one of my own sons have already profited by their friendship with certain of their masters in school or college. I certainly profited by my friendship with one of my tutors, Mr. Cutler; and in Harvard I owed much to the professor of English, Mr. A. S. Hill. Doubtless through my own fault, I saw almost nothing of President Eliot and very little of the professors. I ought to have gained much more than I did gain from writing the themes and forensics. My failure to do so may have been partly due to my taking no interest in the subjects. Before I left Harvard I was already writing one or two chapters of a book I afterwards published on the Naval War of 1812. Those chapters were so dry that they would have made a dictionary seem light reading by comparison. Still, they represented purpose and serious interest on my part, not the perfunctory effort to do well enough to get a certain mark; and corrections of them by a skilled older man would have impressed me and have commanded my respectful attention. But I was not sufficiently developed to make myself take an intelligent interest in some of the subjects assigned me—the character of the Gracchi, for instance. A very clever and studious lad would no doubt have done so, but I personally did not grow up to this particular subject until a good many years later. The frigate and sloop actions between the American and British sea-tigers of 1812 were much more within my grasp. I worked drearily at the Gracchi because I had to; my conscientious and much-to-be-pitied professor dragging me through the theme by main strength, with my feet firmly planted in dull and totally idea-proof resistance.

I had at the time no idea of going into public life, and I never studied elocution or practiced debating. This was a loss to me in one way. In another way it was not. Personally I have not the slightest sympathy with debating contests in which each side is arbitrarily assigned a given proposition and told to maintain it without the least reference to

whether those maintaining it believe in it or not. I know
that under our system this is necessary for lawyers, but I
emphatically disbelieve in it as regards general discussion of
political, social, and industrial matters. What we need is to
turn out of our colleges young men with ardent convictions
on the side of the right; not young men who can make a
good argument for either right or wrong as their interest
bids them. The present method of carrying on debates on
such subjects as "Our Colonial Policy," or "The Need of a
Navy," or "The Proper Position of the Courts in
Constitutional Questions," encourages precisely the wrong
attitude among those who take part in them. There is no
effort to instill sincerity and intensity of conviction. On the
contrary, the net result is to make the contestants feel that
their convictions have nothing to do with their arguments.
I am sorry I did not study elocution in college; but I am
exceedingly glad that I did not take part in the type of
debate in which stress is laid, not upon getting a speaker to
think rightly, but on getting him to talk glibly on the side to
which he is assigned, without regard either to what his
convictions are or to what they ought to be.

I was a reasonably good student in college, standing
just within the first tenth of my class, if I remember rightly;
although I am not sure whether this means the tenth of the
whole number that entered or of those that graduated. I was
given a Phi Beta Kappa "key." My chief interests were
scientific. When I entered college, I was devoted to out-of-
doors natural history, and my ambition was to be a scientific
man of the Audubon, or Wilson, or Baird, or Coues type—
a man like Hart Merriam, or Frank Chapman, or

Hornaday, today. My father had from the earliest days instilled into me the knowledge that I was to work and to make my own way in the world, and I had always supposed that this meant that I must enter business. But in my freshman year (he died when I was a sophomore) he told me that if I wished to become a scientific man I could do so. He explained that I must be sure that I really intensely desired to do scientific work, because if I went into it I must make it a serious career; that he had made enough money to enable me to take up such a career and do non-remunerative work of value if I intended to do the very best work there was in me; but that I must not dream of taking it up as a dilettante. He also gave me a piece of advice that I have always remembered, namely, that, if I was not going to earn money, I must even things up by not spending it. As he expressed it, I had to keep the fraction constant, and if I was not able to increase the numerator, then I must reduce the denominator. In other words, if I went into a scientific career, I must definitely abandon all thought of the enjoyment that could accompany a money-making career, and must find my pleasures elsewhere.

After this conversation I fully intended to make science my life-work. I did not, for the simple reason that at that time Harvard, and I suppose our other colleges, utterly ignored the possibilities of the faunal naturalist, the outdoor naturalist and observer of nature. They treated biology as purely a science of the laboratory and the microscope, a science whose adherents were to spend their time in the study of minute forms of marine life, or else in section-cutting and the study of the tissues of the higher organisms under the microscope. This attitude was, no doubt, in part due to the fact that in most colleges then there was a not always intelligent copying of what was done in the great German universities. The sound revolt against superficiality of study had been carried to an extreme; thoroughness in minutiæ as the only end of study had been erected into a fetish. There was a total failure to understand the great variety of kinds of work that could be done by naturalists, including what could be done by outdoor naturalists—the kind of work which Hart Merriam and his assistants in the Biological Survey have carried to such a high degree of perfection as regards North American mammals. In the entirely proper desire to be thorough and to avoid slipshod methods, the tendency was to treat as not serious, as unscientific, any kind of work that was not carried on with laborious minuteness in the laboratory. My taste was specialized in a totally different direction, and I had no more desire or ability to be a microscopist and section-cutter than to be a mathematician. Accordingly I abandoned all thought of becoming a scientist. Doubtless this meant that I really did not have the intense devotion to science which I thought I had; for, if I had possessed such devotion, I would have carved out a career for myself somehow without regard to discouragements.

As regards political economy, I was of course while in college taught the laissez-faire doctrines—one of them being free trade—then accepted as canonical. Most American boys of my age were taught both by their surroundings and by their studies certain principles which were very valuable from the standpoint of National interest, and certain others which were very much the reverse. The political economists were not especially to blame for this; it was the general attitude of the writers who wrote for us of that generation. Take my beloved Our Young Folks, the magazine of which I have already spoken, and which taught me much more than any of my text-books. Everything in this magazine instilled the individual virtues, and the necessity of character as the chief factor in any man's success-a teaching in which I now believe as sincerely as ever, for all the laws that the wit of man can devise will never make a man a worthy citizen unless he has within himself the right stuff, unless he has self-reliance, energy, courage, the power of insisting on his own rights and the sympathy that makes him regardful of the rights of others. All this individual morality I was taught by the books I read at home and the books I studied at Harvard. But there was almost no teaching of the need for collective action, and of the fact that in addition to, not as a substitute for, individual responsibility, there is a collective responsibility. Books such as Herbert Croly's "Promise of American Life" and Walter E. Weyl's "New Democracy" would generally at that time have been treated either as unintelligible or else as pure heresy.

The teaching which I received was genuinely democratic in one way. It was not so democratic in another. I grew into manhood thoroughly imbued with the feeling that a man must be respected for what he made of himself. But I had also, consciously or unconsciously, been taught that socially and industrially pretty much the whole duty of the man lay in thus making the best of himself; that he should be honest in his dealings with others and charitable in the old-fashioned way to the unfortunate; but that it was no part of his business to join with others in trying to make things better for the many by curbing the abnormal and excessive development of individualism in a few. Now I do not mean that this training was by any means all bad. On the contrary, the insistence upon individual responsibility was, and is, and always will be, a prime necessity. Teaching of the kind I absorbed from both my text-books and my surroundings is a healthy anti-scorbutic to the sentimentality which by complacently excusing the individual for all his shortcomings would finally hopelessly weaken the spring of moral purpose. It also keeps alive that virile vigor for the lack of which in the average individual no possible perfection of law or of community action can ever atone. But such teaching, if not corrected by other teaching, means acquiescence in a riot of lawless business individualism which would be quite as destructive to real civilization as the lawless military individualism of the Dark Ages. I left college and entered the big world owing more than I can express to the training I had received, especially in my own home; but with much else also to learn if I were to become really fitted to do my part in the work that lay ahead for the generation of Americans to which I belonged.

With soul of flame and temper of steel we must act as our coolest judgment bids us. We must exercise the largest charity towards the wrong-doer that is compatible with relentless war against the wrong-doing. We must be just to others, generous to others, and yet we must realize that it is a shameful and a wicked thing not to withstand oppression with high heart and ready hand. With gentleness and tenderness there must go dauntless bravery and grim acceptance of labor and hardship and peril. All for each, and each for all, is a good motto; but only on condition that each works with might and main to so maintain himself as not to be a burden to others.

—Teddy Roosevelt

The Vigor of Life

The following chapter, originally published in Theodore Roosevelt: An Autobiography, *contains rich insights into the genesis of Teddy's belief in what he would later call "the strenuous life." It is the testimony of a man for whom perseverence was a way of life.*—D.W.P.

Looking back, a man really has a more objective feeling about himself as a child than he has about his father or mother. He feels as if that child were not the present he, individually, but an ancestor; just as much an ancestor as either of his parents. The saying that the child is the father to the man may be taken in a sense almost the reverse of that usually given to it. The child is father to the man in the sense that his individuality is separate from the individuality of the grown-up into which he turns. This is perhaps one reason why a man can speak of his childhood and early youth with a sense of detachment.

Having been a sickly boy, with no natural bodily prowess, and having lived much at home, I was at first quite unable to hold my own when thrown into contact with other boys of rougher antecedents. I was nervous and timid. Yet from reading of the people I admired—ranging from the soldiers of Valley Forge, and Morgan's riflemen, to the heroes of my favorite stories-and from hearing of the feats performed by my Southern forefathers and kinsfolk, and from knowing my father, I felt a great admiration for men who were fearless and who could hold their own in the world, and I had a great desire to be like them. Until I was nearly fourteen I let this desire take no more definite shape than day-dreams. Then an incident happened that did me real good. Having an attack of asthma, I was sent off by myself to Moosehead Lake. On the stage-coach ride thither I encountered a couple of other boys who were about my own age, but very much more competent and also much more mischievous. I have no doubt they were good-hearted boys, but they were boys! They found that I was a foreordained and predestined victim, and industriously proceeded to make life miserable for me. The worst feature was that when I finally tried to fight them I discovered that either one singly could not only handle me with easy contempt, but handle me so as not to hurt me much and yet to prevent my doing any damage whatever in return.

The experience taught me what probably no amount of good advice could have taught me. I made up my mind that I must try to learn so that I would not again be put in such a helpless position; and having become quickly and bitterly conscious that I did not have the natural prowess to hold my own, I decided that I would try to supply its place by training. Accordingly, with my father's hearty approval, I started to learn to box. I was a painfully slow and awkward pupil, and certainly worked two or three years before I made any perceptible improvement whatever. My first boxing-master was John Long, an ex-prize-fighter. I can see his rooms now, with colored pictures of the fights between Tom Hyer and Yankee Sullivan, and Heenan and Sayers, and other great events in the annals of the squared circle. On one occasion, to excite interest among his patrons, he held a series of "championship" matches for the different weights, the prizes being, at least in my own class, pewter mugs of a value, I should suppose, approximating fifty cents. Neither he nor I had any idea that I could do anything, but I was entered in the lightweight contest, in which it happened that I was pitted in succession against a couple of reedy striplings who were even worse than I was. Equally to their surprise and to my own, and to John Long's, I won, and the pewter mug became one of my most prized possessions. I kept it, and alluded to it, and I fear bragged about it, for a number of years, and I only wish I knew where it was now. Years later I read an account of a little man who once in a fifth-rate handicap race won a worthless pewter medal and joyed in it ever after. Well, as soon as I read that story I felt that that little man and I were brothers.

This was, as far as I remember, the only one of my exceedingly rare athletic triumphs which would be worth relating. I did a good deal of boxing and wrestling in Harvard, but never attained to the first rank in either, even at my own weight. Once, in the big contests in the Gym, I got either into the finals or semi-finals, I forgot which; but aside from this the chief part I played was to act as trial horse for some friend or classmate who did have a chance of distinguishing himself in the championship contests.

I was fond of horseback-riding, but I took to it slowly and with difficulty, exactly as with boxing. It was a long time before I became even a respectable rider, and I never got much higher. I mean by this that I never became a first-flight man in the hunting field, and never even approached the bronco-busting class in the West. Any man, if he chooses, can gradually school himself to the requisite nerve, and gradually learn the requisite seat and hands, that will enable him to do respectably across country, or to perform the average work on a ranch. Of my ranch experiences I shall speak later. At intervals after leaving college I hunted on Long Island with the Meadowbrook hounds. Almost the only experience I ever had in this connection that was of any interest was on one occasion when I broke my arm. My purse did not permit me to own expensive horses. On this occasion I was riding an animal, a buggy horse originally, which its owner sold because now and then it insisted on thoughtfully lying down when in harness. It never did this under the saddle; and when he turned it out to grass it would solemnly hop over the fence and get somewhere where it did not belong. The last trait was what converted it into a hunter. It was a natural jumper, although without any speed. On the hunt in question I got along very well until the pace winded my ex-buggy horse, and it turned a somersault over a fence. When I got on it after the fall I found I could not use my left arm. I supposed it was merely a strain. The buggy horse was a sedate animal which I rode with a snaffle. So we pounded along at the tail of the hunt, and I did not appreciate that my arm was broken for three or four fences. Then we came to a big drop, and the jar made the bones slip past one another so as to throw the hand out of position. It did not hurt me at all, and as the horse was as easy to sit as a rocking-chair, I got in at the death.

I think August Belmont was master of the hunt when the above incident occurred. I know he was master on another occasion on which I met with a mild adventure. On one of the hunts when I was out a man was thrown, dragged by one stirrup, and killed. In consequence I bought a pair of safety stirrups, which I used the next time I went out. Within five minutes after the run began I found that the stirrups were so very "safe" that they would not stay in at all. First one went off at one jump, and then the other at another jump-with a fall for me on each occasion. I hated to give up the fun so early, and accordingly finished the run without any stirrups. My horse never went as fast as on that run. Doubtless a first-class horseman can ride as well without stirrups as with them. But I was not a first-class horseman. When anything unexpected happened, I was apt to clasp the solemn buggy horse firmly with my spurred heels, and the result was that he laid himself out to do his best in the way of galloping. He speedily found that, thanks to the snaffle bit, I could not pull him in, so when we came to a down grade he would usually put on steam. Then if there was a fence at the bottom and he checked at all, I was apt to shoot forward, and in such event we went over the fence in a way that reminded me of Leech's picture, in *Punch*, of Mr. Tom Noddy and his mare jumping a fence in the following order: Mr. Tom Noddy, I; his mare, II. However, I got in at the death this time also.

I was fond of walking and climbing. As a lad I used to go to the north woods, in Maine, both in fall and winter. There I made life friends of two men, Will Dow and Bill Sewall: I canoed with them, and tramped through the woods with them, visiting the winter logging camps on snow-shoes. Afterward they were with me in the West. Will Dow is dead. Bill Sewall was collector of customs under me, on the Aroostook border. Except when hunting I never did any mountaineering save for a couple of conventional trips up the Matterhorn and the Jungfrau on one occasion when I was in Switzerland.

I never did much with the shotgun, but I practiced a good deal with the rifle. I had a rifle-range at Sagamore Hill, where I often took friends to shoot. Once or twice when I was visited by parties of released Boer prisoners, after the close of the South African War, they and I held shooting matches together. The best man with both pistol and rifle who ever shot there was Stewart Edward White. Among the many other good men was a stanch friend, Baron Speck von Sternberg, afterwards German Ambassador at Washington during my Presidency. He was a capital shot, rider, and walker, a devoted and most efficient servant of Germany, who had fought with distinction in the Franco-German War when barely more than a boy; he was the hero of the story of "the pig dog" in Archibald Forbes's volume of reminiscences. It was he who first talked over with me the raising of a regiment of horse riflemen from among the ranchmen and cowboys of the plains. When Ambassador, the poor, gallant, tender-hearted fellow was dying of a slow and painful disease, so that he could not play with the rest of us, but the agony of his mortal illness never in the slightest degree interfered with his work. Among the other men who shot and rode and walked with me was Cecil Spring-Rice, who has just been appointed British Ambassador to the United States. He was my groomsman, my best man, when I was married—at St. George's, Hanover Square, which made me feel as if I were living in one of Thackeray's novels.

My own experience as regards marksmanship was much the same as my experience as regards horsemanship. There are men whose eye and hand are so quick and so sure that they achieve a perfection of marksmanship to which no practice will enable ordinary men to attain. There are other men who cannot learn to shoot with any accuracy at all. In between come the mass of men of ordinary abilities who, if they choose resolutely to practice, can by sheer industry and judgment make themselves fair rifle shots. The men who show this requisite industry and judgment can without special difficulty raise themselves to the second class of respectable rifle shots; and it is to this class that I belong. But to have reached this point of marksmanship with the rifle at a target by no means implies ability to hit game in the field, especially dangerous game. All kinds of other qualities, moral and physical, enter into being a good hunter, and especially a good hunter after dangerous game, just as all kinds of other qualities in addition to skill with the rifle enter into being a good soldier. With dangerous game, after a fair degree of efficiency with the rifle has been attained, the prime requisites are cool judgment and that kind of nerve which consists in avoiding being rattled. Any beginner is apt to have "buck fever," and therefore no beginner should go at dangerous game.

Buck fever means a state of intense nervous excitement which may be entirely divorced from timidity. It may affect a man the first time he has to speak to a large audience just as it affects him the first time he sees a buck or goes into battle. What such a man needs is not courage but nerve control, cool-headedness. This he can get only by actual practice. He must, by custom and repeated exercise of self-mastery, get his nerves thoroughly under control. This is largely a matter of habit, in the sense of repeated effort and repeated exercise of will power. If the man has the right stuff in him, his will grows stronger and stronger with each exercise of it—and if he has not the right stuff in him he had better keep clear of dangerous game hunting, or indeed of any other form of sport or work in which there is bodily peril.

After he has achieved the ability to exercise wariness and judgment and the control over his nerves which will make him shoot as well at the game as at a target, he can begin his essays at dangerous game hunting, and he will then find that it does not demand such abnormal prowess as the outsider is apt to imagine. A man who can hit a soda-water bottle at the distance of a few yards can brain a lion or a bear or an elephant at that distance, and if he cannot brain it when it charges he can at least bring it to a standstill. All he has to do is to shoot as accurately as he would at a soda-water bottle; and to do this requires nerve, at least as much as it does physical address. Having reached this point, the hunter must not imagine that he is warranted in taking desperate chances. There are degrees in proficiency; and what is a warrantable and legitimate risk for a man to take when he has reached a certain grade of efficiency may be a foolish risk for him to take before he has reached that grade. A man who has reached the degree of proficiency indicated above is quite warranted in walking in at a lion at bay, in an open plain, to, say, within a hundred yards. If the lion has not charged, the man ought at that distance to knock him over and prevent his charging; and if the lion is already charging, the man ought at that distance to be able to stop him. But the amount of prowess which warrants a man in relying on his ability to perform this feat does not by any means justify him in thinking that, for instance, he can crawl after a wounded lion into thick cover. I have known men of indifferent prowess to perform this latter feat successfully, but at least as often they have been unsuccessful, and in these cases the result has been unpleasant. The man who habitually follows wounded lions into thick cover must be a hunter of the highest skill, or he can count with certainty on an ultimate mauling.

The first two or three bucks I ever saw gave me buck fever badly, but after I had gained experience with ordinary game I never had buck fever at all with dangerous game. In my case the overcoming of buck fever was the result of conscious effort and a deliberate determination to overcome it. More happily constituted men never have to make this determined effort at all—which may perhaps show that the average man can profit more from my experiences than he can from those of the exceptional man.

I have shot only five kinds of animals which can fairly be called dangerous game—that is, the lion, elephant, rhinoceros, and buffalo in Africa, and the big grizzly bear a quarter of a century ago in the Rockies. Taking into account not only my own personal experience, but the experiences of many veteran hunters, I regard all the four African animals, but especially the lion, elephant, and buffalo, as much more dangerous than the grizzly. As it happened, however, the only narrow escape I personally ever had was from a grizzly, and in Africa the animal killed closest to me as it was charging was a rhinoceros-all of which goes to show that a man must not generalize too broadly from his own personal experiences. On the whole, I think the lion the most dangerous of all these five animals; that is, I think that, if fairly hunted, there is a larger percentage of hunters killed or mauled for a given number of lions killed than for a given number of any one of the other animals. Yet I personally had no difficulties with lions. I twice killed lions which were at bay and just starting to charge, and I killed a heavy-maned male while it was in full charge. But in each instance I had plenty of leeway, the animal being so far off that even if my bullet had not been fatal I should have had time for a couple more shots. The African buffalo is undoubtedly a dangerous beast, but it happened that the few that I shot did not charge. A bull elephant, a vicious "rogue," which had been killing people in the native villages, did charge before being shot at. My son Kermit and I stopped it at forty yards. Another bull elephant, also unwounded, which charged, nearly got me, as I had just fired both cartridges from my heavy double-barreled rifle in killing the bull I was after—the first wild elephant I had ever seen. The second bull came through the thick brush to my left like a steam plow through a light snowdrift, everything snapping before his rush, and was so near that he could have hit me with his trunk. I slipped past him behind a tree. People have asked me how I felt on this occasion. My answer has always been that I suppose I felt as most men of like experience feel on such occasions. At such a moment a hunter is so very busy that he has no time to get frightened. He wants to get in his cartridges and try another shot.

Rhinoceros are truculent, blustering beasts, much the most stupid of all the dangerous game I know. Generally their attitude is one of mere stupidity and bluff. But on occasions they do charge wickedly, both when wounded and when entirely unprovoked. The first I ever shot I mortally wounded at a few rods' distance, and it charged with the utmost determination, whereat I and my companion both fired, and more by good luck than anything else brought it to the ground just thirteen paces from where we stood. Another rhinoceros may or may not have been meaning to charge me; I have never been certain which. It heard us and came at us through rather thick brush, snorting and tossing its head. I am by no means sure that it had fixedly hostile intentions, and indeed with my present experience I think it likely that if I had not fired it would have flinched at the last moment and either retreated or gone by me. But I am not a rhinoceros mind reader, and its actions were such as to warrant my regarding it as a suspicious character. I stopped it with a couple of bullets, and then followed it up and killed it. The skins of all these animals which I thus killed are in the National Museum at Washington.

But, as I said above, the only narrow escape I met with was not from one of these dangerous African animals, but from a grizzly bear. It was about twenty-four years ago. I had wounded the bear just at sunset, in a wood of lodge-pole pines, and, following him, I wounded him again, as he stood on the other side of a thicket. He then charged through the brush, coming with such speed and with such an irregular gait that, try as I would, I was not able to get the sight of my rifle on the brain-pan, though I hit him very hard with both the remaining barrels of my magazine Winchester. It was in the days of black powder, and the smoke hung. After my last shot, the first thing I saw was the bear's left paw as he struck at me, so close that I made a quick movement to one side. He was, however, practically already dead, and after another jump, and while in the very act of trying to turn to come at me, he collapsed like a shot rabbit.

By the way, I had a most exasperating time trying to bring in his skin. I was alone, traveling on foot with one very docile little mountain mare for a pack pony. The little mare cared nothing for bears or anything else, so there was no difficulty in packing her. But the man without experience can hardly realize the work it was to get that bearskin off the carcass and then to pack it, wet, slippery, and heavy, so that it would ride evenly on the pony. I was at the time fairly well versed in packing with a "diamond hitch," the standby of Rocky Mountain packers in my day; but the diamond hitch is a two-man job; and even working with a "squaw hitch," I got into endless trouble with that wet and slippery bearskin. With infinite labor I would get the skin on the pony and run the ropes over it until to all seeming it was fastened properly. Then off we would start, and after going about a hundred yards I would notice the hide beginning to bulge through between two ropes. I would shift one of them, and then the hide would bulge somewhere else. I would shift the rope again; and still the hide would flow slowly out as if it was lava. The first thing I knew it would come down on one side, and the little mare, with her feet planted resolutely, would wait for me to perform my part by getting that bearskin back in its proper place on the McClellan saddle which I was using as a makeshift pack saddle. The feat of killing the bear the previous day sank into nothing compared with the feat of making the bearskin ride properly as a pack on the following three days.

The reason why I was alone in the mountains on this occasion was because, for the only time in all my experience, I had a difficulty with my guide. He was a crippled old mountain man, with a profound contempt for "tenderfeet," a contempt that in my case was accentuated by the fact that I wore spectacles—which at that day and in that region were usually held to indicate a defective moral character in the wearer. He had never previously acted as guide, or, as he expressed it, "trundled a tenderfoot," and though a good hunter, who showed me much game, our experience together was not happy. He was very rheumatic and liked to lie abed late, so that I usually had to get breakfast, and, in fact, do most of the work around camp. Finally one day he declined to go out with me, saying that he had a pain. When, that afternoon, I got back to camp, I speedily found what the "pain" was. We were traveling very light indeed, I having practically nothing but my buffalo sleeping-bag, my wash kit, and a pair of socks. I had also taken a flask of whisky for emergencies—although, as I found that the emergencies never arose and that tea was better than whisky when a man was cold or done out, I abandoned the practice of taking whisky on hunting trips twenty years ago. When I got back to camp the old fellow was sitting on a tree-trunk, very erect, with his rifle across his knees, and in response to my nod of greeting he merely leered at me. I leaned my rifle against a tree, walked over to where my bed was lying, and, happening to rummage in it for something, I found the whisky flask was empty. I turned on him at once and accused him of having drunk it, to which he merely responded by asking what I was going to do about it. There did not seem much to do, so I said that we would part company—we were only four or five days from a settlement—and I would go in alone, taking one of the horses. He responded by cocking his rifle and saying that I could go alone and be damned to me, but I could not take any horse. I answered "all right," that if I could not I could not, and began to move around to get some flour and salt pork. He was misled by my quietness and by the fact that I had not in any way resented either his actions or his language during the days we had been together, and did not watch me as closely as he ought to have done. He was sitting with the cocked rifle across his knees, the muzzle to the left. My rifle was leaning against a tree near the cooking things to his right. Managing to get near it, I whipped it up and threw the bead on him, calling, "Hands up!" He of course put up his hands, and then said, "Oh, come, I was only joking;" to which I answered, "Well, I am not. Now straighten your legs and let your rifle go to the ground." He remonstrated, saying the rifle would go off, and I told him to let it go off. However, he straightened his legs in such fashion that it came to the ground without a jar. I then made him move back, and picked up the rifle. By this time he was quite sober, and really did not seem angry, looking at me quizzically. He told me that if I would give him back his rifle, he would call it quits and we could go on together. I did not think it best to trust him, so I told him that our hunt was pretty well through, anyway, and that I would go home. There was a blasted pine on the trail, in plain view of the camp, about a mile off, and I told him that I would leave his rifle at that blasted pine if I could see him in camp, but that he must not come after me, for if he did I should assume that it was with hostile intent and would shoot. He said he had no intention of coming after me; and as he was very much crippled with rheumatism, I did not believe he would do so.

Accordingly I took the little mare, with nothing but some flour, bacon, and tea, and my bed-roll, and started off. At the blasted pine I looked round, and as I could see him in camp, I left his rifle there. I then traveled till dark, and that night, for the only time in my experience, I used in camping a trick of the old-time trappers in the Indian days. I did not believe I would be followed, but still it was not possible to be sure, so, after getting supper, while my pony fed round, I left the fire burning, repacked the mare and pushed ahead until it literally became so dark that I could not see. Then I picketed the mare, slept where I was without a fire until the first streak of dawn, and then pushed on for a couple of hours before halting to take breakfast and to let the little mare have a good feed. No plainsman needs to be told that a man should not lie near a fire if there is danger of an enemy creeping up on him, and that above all a man should not put himself in a position where he can be ambushed at dawn. On this second day I lost the trail, and toward nightfall gave up the effort to find it, camped where I was, and went out to shoot a grouse for supper. It was while hunting in vain for a grouse that I came on the bear and killed it as above described.

When I reached the settlement and went into the store, the storekeeper identified me by remarking: "You're the tenderfoot that old Hank was trundling, ain't you?" I admitted that I was. A good many years later, after I had been elected Vice-President, I went on a cougar hunt in northwestern Colorado with Johnny Goff, a famous hunter and mountain man. It was midwinter. I was rather proud of my achievements, and pictured myself as being known to the few settlers in the neighborhood as a successful mountain-lion hunter. I could not help grinning when I found out that they did not even allude to me as the Vice-President-elect, let alone as a hunter, but merely as "Johnny Goff's tourist."

Of course during the years when I was most busy at serious work I could do no hunting, and even my riding was of a decorous kind. But a man whose business is sedentary should get some kind of exercise if he wishes to keep himself in as good physical trim as his brethren who do manual labor. When I worked on a ranch, I needed no form of exercise except my work, but when I worked in an office the case was different. A couple of summers I played polo with some of my neighbors. I shall always believe we played polo in just the right way for middle-aged men with stables of the general utility order. Of course it was polo which was chiefly of interest to ourselves, the only onlookers being the members of our faithful families. My two ponies were the only occupants of my stable except a cart-horse. My wife and I rode and drove them, and they were used for household errands and for the children, and for two afternoons a week they served me as polo ponies. Polo is a good game, infinitely better for vigorous men than tennis or golf or anything of that kind. There is all the fun of football, with the horse thrown in; and if only people would be willing to play it in simple fashion it would be almost as much within their reach as golf. But at Oyster Bay our great and permanent amusements were rowing and sailing; I do not care for the latter, and am fond of the former. I suppose it sounds archaic, but I cannot help thinking that the people with motor boats miss a great deal. If they would only keep to rowboats or canoes, and use oar or paddle themselves, they would get infinitely more benefit than by having their work done for them by gasoline. But I rarely took exercise merely as exercise. Primarily I took it because I liked it. Play should never be allowed to interfere with work; and a life devoted merely to play is, of all forms of existence, the most dismal. But the joy of life is a very good thing, and while work is the essential in it, play also has its place.

When obliged to live in cities, I for a long time found that boxing and wrestling enabled me to get a good deal of exercise in condensed and attractive form. I was reluctantly obliged to abandon both as I grew older. I dropped the wrestling earliest. When I became Governor, the champion middleweight wrestler of America happened to be in Albany, and I got him to come round three or four afternoons a week. Incidentally I may mention that his presence caused me a difficulty with the Comptroller, who refused to audit a bill I put in for a wrestling-mat, explaining that I could have a billiard-table, billiards being recognized as a proper Gubernatorial amusement, but that a wrestling-mat symbolized something unusual and unheard of and could not be permitted. The middleweight champion was of course so much better than I was that he could not only take care of himself but of me too and see that I was not hurt—for wrestling is a much more violent amusement than boxing. But after a couple of months he had to go away, and he left as a substitute a good-humored, stalwart professional oarsman. The oarsman turned out to know very little about wrestling. He could not even take care of himself, not to speak of me. By the end of our second afternoon one of his long ribs had been caved in and two of my short ribs badly damaged, and my left shoulder-blade so nearly shoved out of place that it creaked. He was nearly as pleased as I was when I told him I thought we would "vote the war a failure" and abandon wrestling. After that I took up boxing again. While President I used to box with some of the aides, as well as play single-stick with General Wood. After a few years I had to abandon boxing as well as wrestling, for in one bout a young captain of artillery cross-countered me on the eye, and the blow smashed the little blood-vessels. Fortunately it was my left eye, but the sight has been dim ever since, and if it had been the right eye I should have been entirely unable to shoot.

Accordingly I thought it better to acknowledge that I had become an elderly man and would have to stop boxing. I then took up jiu-jitsu for a year or two.

When I was in the Legislature and was working very hard, with little chance of getting out of doors, all the exercise I got was boxing and wrestling. A young fellow turned up who was a second-rate prize-fighter, the son of one of my old boxing teachers. For several weeks I had him come round to my rooms in the morning to put on the gloves with me for half an hour. Then he suddenly stopped, and some days later I received a letter of woe from him from the jail. I found that he was by profession a burglar, and merely followed boxing as the amusement of his lighter moments, or when business was slack.

Naturally, being fond of boxing, I grew to know a good many prize-fighters, and to most of those I knew I grew genuinely attached. I have never been able to sympathize with the outcry against prize-fighters. The only objection I have to the prize ring is the crookedness that has attended its commercial development. Outside of this I regard boxing, whether professional or amateur, as a first-class sport, and I do not regard it as brutalizing. Of course matches can be conducted under conditions that make them brutalizing. But this is true of football games and of most other rough and vigorous sports. Most certainly prize-fighting is not half as brutalizing or demoralizing as many forms of big business and of the legal work carried on in connection with big business. Powerful, vigorous men of strong animal development must have some way in which their animal spirits can find vent. When I was Police

Commissioner I found (and Jacob Riis will back me up in this) that the establishment of a boxing club in a tough neighborhood always tended to do away with knifing and gun-fighting among the young fellows who would otherwise have been in murderous gangs. Many of these young fellows were not naturally criminals at all, but they had to have some outlet for their activities. In the same way I have always regarded boxing as a first-class sport to encourage in the Young Men's Christian Association. I do not like to see young Christians with shoulders that slope like a champagne bottle. Of course boxing should be encouraged in the army and navy. I was first drawn to two naval chaplains, Fathers Chidwick and Rainey, by finding that each of them had bought half a dozen sets of boxing-gloves and encouraged their crews in boxing.

When I was Police Commissioner, I heartily approved the effort to get boxing clubs started in New York on a clean basis. Later I was reluctantly obliged to come to the conclusion that the prize ring had become hopelessly debased and demoralized, and as Governor I aided in the passage of and signed the bill putting a stop to professional boxing for money. This was because some of the prize-fighters themselves were crooked, while the crowd of hangers—on who attended and made up and profited by the matches had placed the whole business on a basis of commercialism and brutality that was intolerable. I shall always maintain that boxing contests themselves make good, healthy sport. It is idle to compare them with bull-fighting; the torture and death of the wretched horses in bull-fighting is enough of itself to blast the sport, no matter how great the skill and prowess shown by the bull-fighters. Any sport in which the death and torture of animals is made to furnish pleasure to the spectators is debasing. There should always be the opportunity provided in a glove fight or bare-fist fight to stop it when one competitor is hopelessly outclassed or too badly hammered. But the men who take part in these fights are hard as nails, and it is not worth while to feel sentimental about their receiving punishment which as a matter of fact they do not mind. Of course the men who look on ought to be able to stand up with the gloves, or without them, themselves; I have scant use for the type of sportsmanship which consists merely in looking on at the feats of some one else.

Some as good citizens as I know are or were prize-fighters. Take Mike Donovan, of New York. He and his family represent a type of American citizenship of which we have a right to be proud. Mike is a devoted temperance man, and can be relied upon for every movement in the interest of good citizenship. I was first intimately thrown with him when I was Police Commissioner. One evening he and I—both in dress suits—attended a temperance meeting of Catholic societies. It culminated in a lively set-to between myself and a Tammany Senator who was a very good fellow, but whose ideas of temperance differed radically from mine, and, as the event proved, from those of the majority of the meeting. Mike evidently regarded himself as my backer—he was sitting on the platform beside me—and I think felt as pleased and interested as if the set-to had been physical instead of merely verbal. Afterward I grew to know him well both while I was Governor and while I was President, and many a time he came on and boxed with me.

Battling Nelson was another stanch friend, and he and I think alike on most questions of political and industrial life; although he once expressed to me some commiseration because, as President, I did not get anything like the money return for my services that he aggregated during the same term of years in the ring. Bob Fitzsimmons was another good friend of mine. He has never forgotten his early skill as a blacksmith, and among the things that I value and always keep in use is a penholder made by Bob out of a horseshoe, with an inscription saying that it is "Made for and presented to President Theodore Roosevelt by his friend and admirer, Robert Fitzsimmons." I have for a long time had the friendship of John L. Sullivan, than whom in his prime no better man ever stepped into the ring. He is now a Massachusetts farmer. John used occasionally to visit me at the White House, his advent always causing a distinct flutter among the waiting Senators and Congressmen. When I went to Africa he presented me with a gold-mounted rabbit's foot for luck. I carried it through my African trip; and I certainly had good luck.

On one occasion one of my prize-fighting friends called on me at the White House on business. He explained that he wished to see me alone, sat down opposite me, and put a very expensive cigar on the desk, saying, "Have a cigar." I thanked him and said I did not smoke, to which he responded, "Put it in your pocket." He then added, "Take another; put both in your pocket." This I accordingly did. Having thus shown at the outset the necessary formal courtesy, my visitor, an old and valued friend, proceeded to explain that a nephew of his had enlisted in the Marine Corps, but had been absent without leave, and was threatened with dishonorable discharge on the ground of desertion. My visitor, a good citizen and a patriotic American, was stung to the quick at the thought of such an incident occurring in his family, and he explained to me that it must not occur, that there must not be the disgrace to the family, although he would be delighted to have the offender "handled rough" to teach him a needed lesson; he added that he wished I would take him and handle him myself, for he knew that I would see that he "got all that was coming to him." Then a look of pathos came into his eyes, and he explained: "That boy I just cannot understand. He was my sister's favorite son, and I always took a special interest in him myself. I did my best to bring him up the way he ought to go. But there was just nothing to be done with him. His tastes were naturally low. He took to music!" What form this debasing taste for music assumed I did not inquire; and I was able to grant my friend's wish.

While in the White House I always tried to get a couple of hours' exercise in the afternoons—sometimes tennis, more often riding, or else a rough cross-country walk, perhaps down Rock Creek, which was then as wild as a stream in the White Mountains, or on the Virginia side along the Potomac. My companions at tennis or on these rides and walks we gradually grew to style the Tennis Cabinet; and then we extended the term to take in many of my old-time Western friends such as Ben Daniels, Seth Bullock, Luther Kelly, and others who had taken part with me in more serious outdoor adventures than walking and riding for pleasure. Most of the men who were oftenest with me on these trips—men like Major-General Leonard Wood; or Major-General Thomas Henry Barry; or Presley Marion Rixey, Surgeon-General of the Navy; or Robert Bacon, who was afterwards Secretary of State; or James Garfield, who was Secretary of the Interior; or Gifford Pinchot, who was chief of the Forest Service—were better men physically than I was; but I could ride and walk well enough for us all thoroughly to enjoy it. Often, especially in the winters and early springs, we would arrange for a point to point walk, not turning aside for anything-for instance, swimming Rock Creek or even the Potomac if it came in our way. Of course under such circumstances we had to arrange that our return to Washington should be when it was dark, so that our appearance might scandalize no one. On several occasions we thus swam Rock Creek in the early spring when the ice was floating thick upon it. If we swam the Potomac, we usually took off our clothes. I remember one such occasion when the French Ambassador, Jusserand, who was a member of the Tennis Cabinet, was along, and, just as we were about to get in to swim, somebody said, "Mr. Ambassador, Mr. Ambassador, you haven't taken off your gloves," to which he promptly responded, "I think I will leave them on; we might meet ladies!"

We liked Rock Creek for these walks because we could do so much scrambling and climbing along the cliffs; there was almost as much climbing when we walked down the Potomac to Washington from the Virginia end of the Chain Bridge. I would occasionally take some big-game friend from abroad, Selous or St. George Littledale or Captain Radclyffe or Paul Niedicke, on these walks. Once I invited an entire class of officers who were attending lectures at the War College to come on one of these walks; I chose a route which gave us the hardest climbing along the rocks and the deepest crossings of the creek; and my army friends enjoyed it hugely—being the right sort, to a man.

On March 1, 1909, three days before leaving the Presidency, various members of the Tennis Cabinet lunched with me at the White House. "Tennis Cabinet" was an elastic term, and of course many who ought to have been at the lunch were, for one reason or another, away from Washington; but, to make up for this, a goodly number of out-of-town honorary members, so to speak, were present—for instance, Seth Bullock; Luther Kelly, better known as Yellowstone Kelly in the days when he was an army scout against the Sioux; and Abernathy, the wolf-hunter. At the end of the lunch Seth Bullock suddenly reached forward, swept aside a mass of flowers which made a centerpiece on the table, and revealed a bronze cougar by Proctor, which was a parting gift to me. The lunch party and the cougar were then photographed on the lawn.

Some of the younger officers who were my constant companions on these walks and rides pointed out to me the condition of utter physical worthlessness into which certain of the elder ones had permitted themselves to lapse, and the very bad effect this would certainly have if ever the army were called into service. I then looked into the matter for myself, and was really shocked at what I found. Many of the older officers were so unfit physically that their condition would have excited laughter, had it not been so serious, to think that they belonged to the military arm of the Government. A cavalry colonel proved unable to keep his horse at a smart trot for even half a mile, when I visited his post; a Major-General proved afraid even to let his horse canter, when he went on a ride with us; and certain otherwise good men proved as unable to walk as if they had been sedentary brokers. I consulted with men like Major-Generals Wood and Bell, who were themselves of fine physique, with bodies fit to meet any demand. It was late in my administration; and we deemed it best only to make a beginning-experience teaches the most inveterate reformer how hard it is to get a totally non-military nation to accept seriously any military improvement. Accordingly, I merely issued directions that each officer should prove his ability to walk fifty miles, or ride one hundred, in three days.

This is, of course, a test which many a healthy middle-aged woman would be able to meet. But a large portion of the press adopted the view that it was a bit of capricious tyranny on my part; and a considerable number of elderly officers, with desk rather than field experience, intrigued with their friends in Congress to have the order annulled. So one day I took a ride of a little over one hundred miles myself, in company with Surgeon-General Rixey and two other officers. The Virginia roads were frozen and in ruts, and in the afternoon and evening there was a storm of snow and sleet; and when it had been thus experimentally shown, under unfavorable conditions, how easy it was to do in one day the task for which the army officers were allowed three days, all open objection ceased. But some bureau chiefs still did as much underhanded work against the order as they dared, and it was often difficult to reach them. In the Marine Corps Captain Leonard, who had lost an arm at Tientsin, with two of his lieutenants did the fifty miles in one day; for they were vigorous young men, who laughed at the idea of treating a fifty-mile walk as over-fatiguing. Well, the Navy Department officials rebuked them, and made them take the walk over again in three days, on the ground that taking it in one day did not comply with the regulations! This seems unbelievable; but Leonard assures me it is true. He did not inform me at the time, being afraid to "get in wrong" with his permanent superiors. If I had known of the order, short work would have been made of the bureaucrat who issued it.

In no country with an army worth calling such is there a chance for a man physically unfit to stay in the service. Our countrymen should understand that every army officer—and every marine officer—ought to be summarily removed from the service unless he is able to undergo far severer tests than those which, as a beginning, I imposed. To follow any other course is to put a premium on slothful incapacity, and to do the gravest wrong to the Nation.

I have mentioned all these experiences, and I could mention scores of others, because out of them grew my philosophy—perhaps they were in part caused by my philosophy—of bodily vigor as a method of getting that vigor of soul without which vigor of the body counts for nothing. The dweller in cities has less chance than the dweller in the country to keep his body sound and vigorous. But he can do so, if only he will take the trouble. Any young lawyer, shopkeeper, or clerk, or shop-assistant can keep himself in good condition if he tries. Some of the best men who have ever served under me in the National Guard and in my regiment were former clerks or floor-walkers. Why, Johnny Hayes, the Marathon victor, and at one time world champion, one of my valued friends and supporters, was a floor-walker in Bloomingdale's big department store. Surely with Johnny Hayes as an example, any young man in a city can hope to make his body all that a vigorous man's body should be.

I once made a speech to which I gave the title "The Strenuous Life." Afterwards I published a volume of essays with this for a title. There were two translations of it which always especially pleased me. One was by a Japanese officer who knew English well, and who had carried the essay all through the Manchurian campaign, and later translated it for the benefit of his countrymen. The other was by an Italian lady, whose brother, an officer in the Italian army who had died on duty in a foreign land, had also greatly liked the article and carried it round with him. In translating the title the lady rendered it in Italian as Vigor di Vita. I thought this translation a great improvement on the original, and have always wished that I had myself used "The Vigor of Life" as a heading to indicate what I was trying to preach, instead of the heading I actually did use.

There are two kinds of success, or rather two kinds of ability displayed in the achievement of success. There is, first, the success either in big things or small things which comes to the man who has in him the natural power to do what no one else can do, and what no amount of training, no perseverance or will power, will enable any ordinary man to do. This success, of course, like every other kind of success, may be on a very big scale or on a small scale. The quality which the man possesses may be that which enables him to run a hundred yards in nine and three-fifths seconds, or to play ten separate games of chess at the same time blindfolded, or to add five columns of figures at once without effort, or to write the "Ode to a Grecian Urn," or to deliver the Gettysburg speech, or to show the ability of Frederick at Leuthen or Nelson at Trafalgar. No amount of training of body or mind would enable any good ordinary man to perform any one of these feats. Of course the proper performance of each implies much previous study or training, but in no one of them is success to be attained save by the altogether exceptional man who has in him the something additional which the ordinary man does not have.

This is the most striking kind of success, and it can be attained only by the man who has in him the quality which separates him in kind no less than in degree from his fellows. But much the commoner type of success in every walk of life and in every species of effort is that which comes to the man who differs from his fellows not by the kind of quality which he possesses but by the degree of development which he has given that quality. This kind of success is open to a large number of persons, if only they seriously determine to achieve it. It is the kind of success which is open to the average man of sound body and fair mind, who has no remarkable mental or physical attributes, but who gets just as much as possible in the way of work out of the aptitudes that he does possess. It is the only kind of success that is open to most of us. Yet some of the greatest successes in history have been those of this second class—when I call it second class I am not running it down in the least, I am merely pointing out that it differs in kind from the first class. To the average man it is probably more useful to study this second type of success than to study the first. From the study of the first he can learn inspiration, he can get uplift and lofty enthusiasm. From the study of the second he can, if he chooses, find out how to win a similar success himself.

I need hardly say that all the successes I have ever won have been of the second type. I never won anything without hard labor and the exercise of my best judgment and careful planning and working long in advance. Having been a rather sickly and awkward boy, I was as a young man at first both nervous and distrustful of my own prowess. I had to train myself painfully and laboriously not merely as regards my body but as regards my soul and spirit.

When a boy I read a passage in one of Marryat's books which always impressed me. In this passage the captain of some small British man-of-war is explaining to the hero how to acquire the quality of fearlessness. He says that at the outset almost every man is frightened when he goes into action, but that the course to follow is for the man to keep such a grip on himself that he can act just as if he was not frightened. After this is kept up long enough it changes from pretense to reality, and the man does in very fact become fearless by sheer dint of practicing fearlessness when he does not feel it. (I am using my own language, not Marryat's.) This was the theory upon which I went. There were all kinds of things of which I was afraid at first, ranging from grizzly bears to "mean" horses and gun-fighters; but by acting as if I was not afraid I gradually ceased to be afraid. Most men can have the same experience if they choose. They will first learn to bear themselves well in trials which they anticipate and which they school themselves in advance to meet. After a while the habit will grow on them, and they will behave well in sudden and unexpected emergencies which come upon them unawares.

It is of course much pleasanter if one is naturally fearless, and I envy and respect the men who are naturally fearless. But it is a good thing to remember that the man who does not enjoy this advantage can nevertheless stand beside the man who does, and can do his duty with the like efficiency, if he chooses to. Of course he must not let his desire take the form merely of a day-dream. Let him dream about being a fearless man, and the more he dreams the better he will be, always provided he does his best to realize the dream in practice. He can do his part honorably and well provided only he sets fearlessness before himself as an ideal, schools himself to think of danger merely as something to be faced and overcome, and regards life itself as he should regard it, not as something to be thrown away, but as a pawn to be promptly hazarded whenever the hazard is warranted by the larger interests of the great game in which we are all engaged.

One of our best naval officers sent me the following letter, after the above had appeared:-

"I note in your Autobiography now being published in the Outlook that you refer to the reasons which led you to establish a physical test for the Army, and to the action you took (your 100-mile ride) to prevent the test being abolished. Doubtless you did not know the following facts:

"1. The first annual navy test of 50 miles in three days was subsequently reduced to 25 miles in two days in each quarter.

"2. This was further reduced to 10 miles each month, which is the present 'test,' and there is danger lest even this utterly insufficient test be abolished.

"I enclose a copy of a recent letter to the Surgeon General which will show our present deplorable condition and the worse condition into which we are slipping back.

"The original test of 50 miles in three days did a very great deal of good. It decreased by thousands of dollars the money expended on street car fare, and by a much greater sum the amount expended over the bar. It eliminated a number of the wholly unfit; it taught officers to walk; it forced them to learn the care of their feet and that of their men; and it improved their general health and was rapidly forming a taste for physical exercise."

The enclosed letter ran in part as follows:-

"I am returning under separate cover 'The Soldiers' Foot and the Military Shoe.'

"The book contains knowledge of a practical character that is valuable for the men who have to march, who have suffered from foot troubles, and who must avoid them in order to attain efficiency.

"The words in capitals express, according to my idea, the gist of the whole matter as regards military men.

"The army officer whose men break down on test gets a black eye. The one whose men show efficiency in this respect gets a bouquet.

"To such men the book is invaluable. There is no danger that they will neglect it. They will actually learn it, for exactly the same reasons that our fellows learn the gunnery instructions-or did learn them before they were withdrawn and burned.

"But, I have not been able to interest a single naval officer in this fine book. They will look at the pictures and say it is a good book, but they won't read it. The marine officers, on the contrary, are very much interested, because they have to teach their men to care for their feet and they must know how to care for their own. But the naval officers feel no such necessity, simply because their men do not have to demonstrate their efficiency by practice marches, and they themselves do not have to do a stunt that will show up their own ignorance and inefficiency in the matter.

"For example, some time ago I was talking with some chaps about shoes—the necessity of having them long enough and wide enough, etc., and one of them said: 'I have no use for such shoes, as I never walk except when I have to, and any old shoes do for the 10-mile-a-month stunt,' so there you are!

"When the first test was ordered, Edmonston (Washington shoe man) told me that he sold more real walking shoes to naval officers in three months than he had in the three preceding years. I know three officers who lost both big-toe nails after the first test, and another who walked nine miles in practice with a pair of heavy walking shoes that were too small and was laid up for three days—could not come to the office. I know plenty of men who after the first test had to borrow shoes from larger men until their feet 'went down' to their normal size.

"This test may have been a bit too strenuous for old hearts (of men who had never taken any exercise), but it was excellent as a matter of instruction and training of handling feet-and in an emergency (such as we soon may have in Mexico) sound hearts are not much good if the feet won't stand.

"However, the 25-mile test in two days each quarter answered the same purpose, for the reason that 12.5 miles will produce sore feet with bad shoes, and sore feet and lame muscles even with good shoes, if there has been no practice marching.

"It was the necessity of doing 12.5 more miles on the second day with sore feet and lame muscles that made 'em sit up and take notice—made 'em practice walking, made 'em avoid street cars, buy proper shoes, show some curiosity about sox and the care of the feet in general.

"All this passed out with the introduction of the last test of 10 miles a month. As one fellow said: 'I can do that in sneakers'—but he couldn't if the second day involved a tramp on the sore feet.

"The point is that whereas formerly officers had to practice walking a bit and give some attention to proper footgear, now they don't have to, and the natural consequence is that they don't do it.

"There are plenty of officers who do not walk any more than is necessary to reach a street car that will carry them from their residences to their offices. Some who have motors do not do so much. They take no exercise. They take cocktails instead and are getting beefy and 'ponchy,' and something should be done to remedy this state of affairs.

"It would not be necessary if service opinion required officers so to order their lives that it would be common knowledge that they were 'hard,' in order to avoid the danger of being selected out.

"We have no such service opinion, and it is not in process of formation. On the contrary, it is known that the 'Principal Dignitaries' unanimously advised the Secretary to abandon all physical tests. He, a civilian, was wise enough not to take the advice.

"I would like to see a test established that would oblige officers to take sufficient exercise to pass it without inconvenience. For the reasons given above, 20 miles in two days every other month would do the business, while 10 miles each month does not touch it, simply because nobody has to walk on 'next day' feet. As for the proposed test of so many hours 'exercise' a week, the flat foots of the pendulous belly muscles are delighted. They are looking into the question of pedometers, and will hang one of these on their wheezy chests and let it count every shuffling step they take out of doors.

"If we had an adequate test throughout 20 years, there

would at the end of that time be few if any sacks of blubber at the upper end of the list; and service opinion against that sort of thing would be established."

These tests were kept during my administration. They were afterwards abandoned; not through perversity or viciousness; but through weakness, and inability to understand the need of preparedness in advance, if the emergencies of war are to be properly met, when, or if, they arrive.

In Cowboyland

The following commentary was written in 1919 by Teddy Roosevelt's friend and the editor of Theodore Roosevelt's Letter's To his Children. Although organized differently, and with different editorial comments, we have included in this volume most of the letters originally published by Mr. Bishop.—D.W.P.

Though I had previously made a trip into the then Territory of Dakota, beyond the Red River, it was not until 1883 that I went to the Little Missouri, and there took hold of two cattle ranches, the Chimney Butte and the Elkhorn.

It was still the Wild West in those days, the Far West, the West of Owen Wister's stories and Frederic Remington's drawings, the West of the Indian and the buffalo-hunter, the soldier and the cow-puncher. That land of the West has gone now, "gone, gone with lost Atlantis," gone to the isle of ghosts and of strange dead memories. It was a land of vast silent spaces, of lonely rivers, and of plains where the wild game stared at the passing horseman. It was a land of scattered ranches, of herds of long-horned cattle, and of reckless riders who unmoved looked in the eyes of life or of death. In that land we led a free and hardy life, with horse and with rifle. We worked under the scorching midsummer sun, when the wide plains shimmered and wavered in the heat; and we knew the freezing misery of riding night guard round the cattle in the late fall round-up. In the soft springtime the stars were glorious in our eyes each night before we fell asleep; and in the winter we rode through blinding blizzards, when the driven snow-dust burned our faces. There were monotonous days, as we guided the trail cattle or the beef herds, hour after hour, at the slowest of walks; and minutes or hours teeming with excitement as we stopped stampedes or swam the herds across rivers treacherous with quicksands or brimmed with running ice. We knew toil and hardship and hunger and thirst; and we saw men die violent deaths as they worked among the horses and cattle, or fought in evil feuds with one another; but we felt the beat of hardy life in our veins, and ours was the glory of work and the joy of living.

It was right and necessary that this life should pass, for the safety of our country lies in its being made the country of the small home-maker. The great unfenced ranches, in the days of "free grass," necessarily represented a temporary stage in our history. The large migratory flocks of sheep, each guarded by the hired shepherds of absentee owners, were the first enemies of the cattlemen; and owing to the way they ate out the grass and destroyed all other vegetation, these roving sheep bands represented little of permanent good to the country. But the homesteaders, the permanent settlers, the men who took up each his own farm on which he lived and brought up his family, these represented from the National standpoint the most desirable of all possible users of, and dwellers on, the soil. Their advent meant the breaking up of the big ranches; and the change was a National gain, although to some of us an individual loss.

I first reached the Little Missouri on a Northern Pacific train about three in the morning of a cool September day in 1883. Aside from the station, the only building was a ramshackle structure called the Pyramid Park Hotel. I dragged my duffle-bag thither, and hammered at the door until the frowsy proprietor appeared, muttering oaths. He ushered me upstairs, where I was given one of the fourteen beds in the room which by itself constituted the entire upper floor. Next day I walked over to the abandoned army post, and, after some hours among the gray log shacks, a ranchman who had driven into the station agreed to take me out to his ranch, the Chimney Butte ranch, where he was living with his brother and their partner.

The ranch was a log structure with a dirt roof, a corral for the horses near by, and a chicken-house jabbed against the rear of the ranch house. Inside there was only one room, with a table, three or four chairs, a cooking-stove, and three bunks. The owners were Sylvane and Joe Ferris and William J. Merrifield. Later all three of them held my commissions while I was President. Merrifield was Marshal of Montana, and as Presidential elector cast the vote of that State for me in 1904; Sylvane Ferris was Land Officer in North Dakota, and Joe Ferris Postmaster at Medora. There was a fourth man, George Meyer, who also worked for me later. That evening we all played old sledge round the table, and at one period the game was interrupted by a frightful squawking outside which told us that a bobcat had made a raid on the chicken-house.

After a buffalo hunt with my original friend, Joe Ferris, I entered into partnership with Merrifield and Sylvane Ferris, and we started a cow ranch, with the maltese cross brand-always known as "maltee cross," by the way, as the general impression along the Little Missouri was that "maltese" must be a plural. Twenty-nine years later my four friends of that night were delegates to the First Progressive National Convention at Chicago. They were among my most constant companions for the few years next succeeding the evening when the bobcat interrupted the game of old sledge. I lived and worked with them on the ranch, and with them and many others like them on the round-up; and I brought out from Maine, in order to start the Elkhorn ranch lower down the river, my two backwoods friends Sewall and Dow. My brands for the lower ranch were the elkhorn and triangle.

I do not believe there ever was any life more attractive to a vigorous young fellow than life on a cattle ranch in those days. It was a fine, healthy life, too; it taught a man self-reliance, hardihood, and the value of instant decision-in short, the virtues that ought to come from life in the open country. I enjoyed the life to the full. After the first year I built on the Elkhorn ranch a long, low ranch house of hewn logs, with a veranda, and with, in addition to the other rooms, a bedroom for myself, and a sitting-room with a big fire-place. I got out a rocking-chair—I am very fond of rocking-chairs—and enough books to fill two or three shelves, and a rubber bathtub so that I could get a bath. And then I do not see how any one could have lived more comfortably. We had buffalo robes and bearskins of our own killing. We always kept the house clean-using the word in a rather large sense. There were at least two rooms that were always warm, even in the bitterest weather; and we had plenty to eat. Commonly the mainstay of every meal was game of our own killing, usually antelope or deer, sometimes grouse or ducks, and occasionally, in the earlier days, buffalo or elk. We also had flour and bacon, sugar, salt, and canned tomatoes. And later, when some of the men married and brought out their wives, we had all kinds of good things, such as jams and jellies made from the wild plums and the buffalo berries, and potatoes from the forlorn little garden patch. Moreover, we had milk. Most ranchmen at that time never had milk. I knew more than one ranch with ten thousand head of cattle where there was not a cow that could be milked. We made up our minds that we would be more enterprising. Accordingly, we started to domesticate some of the cows. Our first effort was not successful, chiefly because we did not devote the needed time and patience to the matter. And we found that to race a cow two miles at full speed on horseback, then rope her, throw her, and turn her upside down to milk her, while exhilarating as a pastime, was not productive of results. Gradually we accumulated tame cows, and, after we had thinned out the bobcats and coyotes, more chickens.

The ranch house stood on the brink of a low bluff overlooking the broad, shallow bed of the Little Missouri, through which at most seasons there ran only a trickle of water, while in times of freshet it was filled brimful with the boiling, foaming, muddy torrent. There was no neighbor for ten or fifteen miles on either side of me. The river twisted down in long curves between narrow bottoms bordered by sheer cliff walls, for the Bad Lands, a chaos of peaks, plateaus, and ridges, rose abruptly from the edges of the level, tree-clad, or grassy, alluvial meadows. In front of the ranch-house veranda was a row of cottonwood trees with gray-green leaves which quivered all day long if there was a breath of air. From these trees came the far-away, melancholy cooing of mourning doves, and little owls perched in them and called tremulously at night. In the long summer afternoons we would sometimes sit on the piazza, when there was no work to be done, for an hour or two at a time, watching the cattle on the sand-bars, and the sharply channeled and strangely carved amphitheater of cliffs across the bottom opposite; while the vultures wheeled overhead, their black shadows gliding across the glaring white of the dry river-bed. Sometimes from the ranch we saw deer, and once when we needed meat I shot one across the river as I stood on the piazza. In the winter, in the days of iron cold, when everything was white under the snow, the river lay in its bed fixed and immovable as a bar of bent steel, and then at night wolves and lynxes traveled up and down it as if it had been a highway passing in front of the ranch house. Often in the late fall or early winter, after a hard day's hunting, or when returning from one of the winter line camps, we did not reach the ranch until hours after sunset; and after the weary tramping in the cold it was keen pleasure to catch the first red gleam of the fire-lit windows across the snowy wastes.

The Elkhorn ranch house was built mainly by Sewall and Dow, who, like most men from the Maine woods, were mighty with the ax. I could chop fairly well for an amateur, but I could not do one-third the work they could. One day when we were cutting down the cottonwood trees, to begin our building operations, I heard some one ask Dow what the total cut had been, and Dow not realizing that I was within hearing, answered: "Well, Bill cut down fifty-three, I cut forty-nine, and the boss he beavered down seventeen." Those who have seen the stump of a tree which has been gnawed down by a beaver will understand the exact force of the comparison.

In those days on a cow ranch the men were apt to be away on the various round-ups at least half the time. It was interesting and exciting work, and except for the lack of sleep on the spring and summer round-ups it was not exhausting work; compared to lumbering or mining or blacksmithing, to sit in the saddle is an easy form of labor. The ponies were of course grass-fed and unshod. Each man had his own string of nine or ten. One pony would be used for the morning work, one for the afternoon, and neither would again be used for the next three days. A separate pony was kept for night riding.

The spring and early summer round-ups were especially for the branding of calves. There was much hard work and some risk on a round-up, but also much fun. The meeting-place was appointed weeks beforehand, and all the ranchmen of the territory to be covered by the round-up sent their representatives. There were no fences in the West that I knew, and their place was taken by the cowboy and the branding-iron. The cattle wandered free. Each calf was branded with the brand of the cow it was following. Sometimes in winter there was what we called line riding; that is, camps were established and the line riders traveled a definite beat across the desolate wastes of snow, to and fro from one camp to another, to prevent the cattle from drifting. But as a rule nothing was done to keep the cattle in any one place. In the spring there was a general round-up in each locality. Each outfit took part in its own round-up, and all the outfits of a given region combined to send representatives to the two or three round-ups that covered the neighborhoods near by into which their cattle might drift. For example, our Little Missouri round-up generally worked down the river from a distance of some fifty or sixty miles above my ranch toward the Kildeer Mountains, about the same distance below. In addition we would usually send representatives to the Yellowstone round-up, and to the round-up along the upper Little Missouri; and, moreover, if we heard that cattle had drifted, perhaps toward the Indian reservation southeast of us, we would send a wagon and rider after them.

At the meeting-point, which might be in the valley of a half-dry stream, or in some broad bottom of the river itself, or perchance by a couple of ponds under some queerly shaped butte that was a landmark for the region round about, we would all gather on the appointed day. The chuck-wagons, containing the bedding and food, each drawn by four horses and driven by the teamster cook, would come jolting and rattling over the uneven sward. Accompanying each wagon were eight or ten riders, the

cow-punchers, while their horses, a band of a hundred or
so, were driven by the two herders, one of whom was
known as the day wrangler and one as the night wrangler.
The men were lean, sinewy fellows, accustomed to riding
half-broken horses at any speed over any country by day or
by night. They wore flannel shirts, with loose
handkerchiefs knotted round their necks, broad hats, high-
heeled boots with jingling spurs, and sometimes leather
shaps, although often they merely had their trousers tucked
into the tops of their high boots. There was a good deal of
rough horse-play, and, as with any other gathering of men
or boys of high animal spirits, the horse-play sometimes
became very rough indeed; and as the men usually carried
revolvers, and as there were occasionally one or two noted
gun-fighters among them, there was now and then a
shooting affray. A man who was a coward or who shirked
his work had a bad time, of course; a man could not afford
to let himself be bullied or treated as a butt; and, on the
other hand, if he was "looking for a fight," he was certain to
find it. But my own experience was that if a man did not talk
until his associates knew him well and liked him, and if he
did his work, he never had any difficulty in getting on. In
my own round-up district I speedily grew to be friends with
most of the men. When I went among strangers I always
had to spend twenty-four hours in living down the fact that
I wore spectacles, remaining as long as I could judiciously
deaf to any side remarks about "four eyes," unless it became
evident that my being quiet was misconstrued and that it
was better to bring matters to a head at once.

If, for instance, I was sent off to represent the Little

Missouri brands on some neighboring round-up, such as the Yellowstone, I usually showed that kind of diplomacy which consists in not uttering one word that can be avoided. I would probably have a couple of days' solitary ride, mounted on one horse and driving eight or ten others before me, one of them carrying my bedding. Loose horses drive best at a trot, or canter, and if a man is traveling alone in this fashion it is a good thing to have them reach the camp ground sufficiently late to make them desire to feed and sleep where they are until morning. In consequence I never spent more than two days on the journey from whatever the point was at which I left the Little Missouri, sleeping the one night for as limited a number of hours as possible.

As soon as I reached the meeting-place I would find out the wagon to which I was assigned. Riding to it, I turned my horses into the saddle-band and reported to the wagon boss, or, in his absence, to the cook-always a privileged character, who was allowed and expected to order men around. He would usually grumble savagely and profanely about my having been put with his wagon, but this was merely conventional on his part; and if I sat down and said nothing he would probably soon ask me if I wanted anything to eat, to which the correct answer was that I was not hungry and would wait until meal-time. The bedding rolls of the riders would be strewn round the grass, and I would put mine down a little outside the ring, where I would not be in any one's way, with my six or eight branding-irons beside it. The men would ride in, laughing and talking with one another, and perhaps nodding to me. One of their number, usually the wagon foreman, might put some question to me as to what brands I represented, but no other word would be addressed to me, nor would I be expected to volunteer any conversation. Supper would consist of bacon, Dutch oven bread, and possibly beef; once I won the good graces of my companions at the outset by appearing with two antelope which I had shot. After supper I would roll up in my bedding as soon as possible, and the others would follow suit at their pleasure.

At three in the morning or thereabouts, at a yell from the cook, all hands would turn hurriedly out. Dressing was a simple affair. Then each man rolled and corded his bedding—if he did not, the cook would leave it behind and he would go without any for the rest of the trip—and came to the fire, where he picked out a tin cup, tin plate, and knife and fork, helped himself to coffee and to whatever food there was, and ate it standing or squatting as best suited him. Dawn was probably breaking by this time, and the trampling of unshod hoofs showed that the night wrangler was bringing in the pony herd. Two of the men would then run ropes from the wagon at right angles to one another, and into this as a corral the horses would be driven. Each man might rope one of his own horses, or more often point it out to the most skillful roper of the outfit, who would rope it for him—for if the man was an unskillful roper and roped the wrong horse or roped the horse in the wrong place there was a chance of the whole herd stampeding. Each man then saddled and bridled his horse. This was usually followed by some resolute bucking on the part of two or three of the horses, especially in the early days of each round-up. The bucking was always a source of amusement to all the men whose horses did not buck, and these fortunate ones would gather round giving ironical advice, and especially adjuring the rider not to "go to leather"—that is, not to steady himself in the saddle by catching hold of the saddle-horn.

As soon as the men had mounted, the whole outfit started on the long circle, the morning circle. Usually the ranch foreman who bossed a given wagon was put in charge of the men of one group by the round-up foreman; he might keep his men together until they had gone some ten or fifteen miles from camp, and then drop them in couples at different points. Each couple made its way toward the wagon, gathering all the cattle it could find. The morning's ride might last six or eight hours, and it was still longer before some of the men got in. Singly and in twos and threes they appeared from every quarter of the horizon, the dust rising from the hoofs of the steers and bulls, the cows and calves, they had collected. Two or three of the men were left to take care of the herd while the others changed horses, ate a hasty dinner, and then came out to the afternoon work. This consisted of each man in succession being sent into the herd, usually with a companion, to cut out the cows of his brand or brands which were followed by unbranded calves, and also to cut out any mavericks or unbranded yearlings. We worked each animal gently out to the edge of the herd, and then with a sudden dash took it off at a run. It was always desperately anxious to break back and rejoin the herd. There was much breakneck galloping and twisting and turning before its desire was thwarted and it was driven to join the rest of the cut—that is, the other animals which had been cut out, and which were being held by one or two other men. Cattle hate being alone, and it was no easy matter to hold the first one or two that were cut out; but soon they got a little herd of their own, and then they were contented. When the cutting out had all been done, the calves were branded, and all misadventures of the "calf wrestlers," the men who seized, threw, and held each calf when roped by the mounted roper, were hailed with yelling laughter. Then the animals which for one reason or another it was desired to drive along with the round-up were put into one herd and left in charge of a couple of night guards, and the rest of us would loaf back to the wagon for supper and bed.

By this time I would have been accepted as one of the rest of the outfit, and all strangeness would have passed off, the attitude of my fellow cow-punchers being one of friendly forgiveness even toward my spectacles. Night guards for the cattle herd were then assigned by the captain of the wagon, or perhaps by the round-up foreman, according to the needs of the case, the guards standing for two hours at a time from eight in the evening till four in the morning. The first and last watches were preferable, because sleep was not broken as in both of the other two. If things went well, the cattle would soon bed down and nothing further would occur until morning, when there was a repetition of the work, the wagon moving each day eight or ten miles to some appointed camping-place.

Each man would picket his night horse near the wagon, usually choosing the quietest animal in his string for that purpose, because to saddle and mount a "mean" horse at night is not pleasant. When utterly tired, it was hard to have to get up for one's trick at night herd. Nevertheless, on ordinary nights the two hours round the cattle in the still darkness were pleasant. The loneliness, under the vast empty sky, and the silence, in which the breathing of the cattle sounded loud, and the alert readiness to meet any emergency which might suddenly arise out of the formless night, all combined to give one a sense of subdued interest. Then, one soon got to know the cattle of marked individuality, the ones that led the others into mischief; and one also grew to recognize the traits they all possessed in common, and the impulses which, for instance, made a whole herd get up towards midnight, each beast turning round and then lying down again. But by the end of the watch each rider had studied the cattle until it grew monotonous, and heartily welcomed his relief guard. A newcomer, of course, had any amount to learn, and sometimes the simplest things were those which brought him to grief.

One night early in my career I failed satisfactorily to identify the direction in which I was to go in order to reach the night herd. It was a pitch-dark night. I managed to get started wrong, and I never found either the herd or the wagon again until sunrise, when I was greeted with withering scorn by the injured cow-puncher, who had been obliged to stand double guard because I failed to relieve him.

There were other misadventures that I met with where the excuse was greater. The punchers on night guard usually rode round the cattle in reverse directions; calling and singing to them if the beasts seemed restless, to keep them quiet. On rare occasions something happened that made the cattle stampede, and then the duty of the riders was to keep with them as long as possible and try gradually to get control of them.

One night there was a heavy storm, and all of us who were at the wagons were obliged to turn out hastily to help the night herders. After a while there was a terrific peal of thunder, the lightning struck right by the herd, and away all the beasts went, heads and horns and tails in the air. For a minute or two I could make out nothing except the dark forms of the beasts running on every side of me, and I should have been very sorry if my horse had stumbled, for those behind would have trodden me down. Then the herd split, part going to one side, while the other part seemingly kept straight ahead, and I galloped as hard as ever beside them. I was trying to reach the point—the leading animals—in order to turn them, when suddenly there was a tremendous splashing in front. I could dimly make out that the cattle immediately ahead and to one side of me were disappearing, and the next moment the horse and I went off a cut bank into the Little Missouri. I bent away back in the saddle, and though the horse almost went down he just recovered himself, and, plunging and struggling through water and quicksand, we made the other side. Here I discovered that there was another cowboy with the same part of the herd that I was with; but almost immediately we separated. I galloped hard through a bottom covered with big cottonwood trees, and stopped the part of the herd that I was with, but very soon they broke on me again, and repeated this twice. Finally toward morning the few I had left came to a halt.

It had been raining hard for some time. I got off my horse and leaned against a tree, but before long the infernal cattle started on again, and I had to ride after them. Dawn came soon after this, and I was able to make out where I was and head the cattle back, collecting other little bunches as I went. After a while I came on a cowboy on foot carrying his saddle on his head. He was my companion of the previous night. His horse had gone full speed into a tree and killed itself, the man, however, not being hurt. I could not help him, as I had all I could do to handle the cattle. When I got them to the wagon, most of the other men had already come in and the riders were just starting on the long circle. One of the men changed my horse for me while I ate a hasty breakfast, and then we were off for the day's work.

As only about half of the night herd had been brought back, the circle riding was particularly heavy, and it was ten hours before we were back at the wagon. We then changed horses again and worked the whole herd until after sunset, finishing just as it grew too dark to do anything more. By this time I had been nearly forty hours in the saddle, changing horses five times, and my clothes had thoroughly dried on me, and I fell asleep as soon as I touched the bedding. Fortunately some men who had gotten in late in the morning had had their sleep during the daytime, so that the rest of us escaped night guard and were not called until four next morning. Nobody ever gets enough sleep on a round-up.

The above was the longest number of consecutive hours I ever had to be in the saddle. But, as I have said, I changed horses five times, and it is a great lightening of labor for a rider to have a fresh horse. Once when with Sylvane Ferris

I spent about sixteen hours on one horse, riding seventy or eighty miles. The round-up had reached a place called the ox-bow of the Little Missouri, and we had to ride there, do some work around the cattle, and ride back.

Another time I was twenty-four hours on horseback in company with Merrifield without changing horses. On this occasion we did not travel fast. We had been coming back with the wagon from a hunting trip in the Big Horn Mountains. The team was fagged out, and we were tired of walking at a snail's pace beside it. When we reached country that the driver thoroughly knew, we thought it safe to leave him, and we loped in one night across a distance which it took the wagon the three following days to cover. It was a beautiful moonlight night, and the ride was delightful. All day long we had plodded at a walk, weary and hot. At supper time we had rested two or three hours, and the tough little riding horses seemed as fresh as ever. It was in September. As we rode out of the circle of the firelight, the air was cool in our faces. Under the bright moonlight, and then under the starlight, we loped and cantered mile after mile over the high prairie. We passed bands of antelope and herds of long-horn Texas cattle, and at last, just as the first red beams of the sun flamed over the bluffs in front of us, we rode down into the valley of the Little Missouri, where our ranch house stood.

I never became a good roper, nor more than an average rider, according to ranch standards. Of course a man on a ranch has to ride a good many bad horses, and is bound to encounter a certain number of accidents, and of these I had my share, at one time cracking a rib, and on another occasion the point of my shoulder. We were hundreds of miles from a doctor, and each time, as I was on the round-up, I had to get through my work for the next few weeks as best I could, until the injury healed of itself. When I had the opportunity I broke my own horses, doing it gently and gradually and spending much time over it, and choosing the horses that seemed gentle to begin with. With these horses I never had any difficulty. But frequently there was neither time nor opportunity to handle our mounts so elaborately. We might get a band of horses, each having been bridled and saddled two or three times, but none of them having been broken beyond the extent implied in this bridling and saddling. Then each of us in succession would choose a horse (for his string), I as owner of the ranch being given the first choice on each round, so to speak. The first time I was ever on a round-up Sylvane Ferris, Merrifield, Meyer, and I each chose his string in this fashion. Three or four of the animals I got were not easy to ride. The effort both to ride them and to look as if I enjoyed doing so, on some cool morning when my grinning cowboy friends had gathered round "to see whether the high-headed bay could buck the boss off," doubtless was of benefit to me, but lacked much of being enjoyable. The time I smashed my rib I was bucked off on a stone. The time I hurt the point of my shoulder I was riding a big, sulky horse named Ben Butler, which went over backwards with me. When we got up it still refused to go anywhere; so, while I sat it, Sylvane Ferris and George Meyer got their ropes on its neck and dragged it a few hundred yards, choking but stubborn, all four feet firmly planted and plowing the ground. When they released the ropes it lay down and wouldn't get up. The round-up had started; so Sylvane gave me his horse, Baldy, which sometimes bucked but never went over backwards, and he got on the now rearisen Ben Butler. To my discomfiture Ben started quietly beside us, while Sylvane remarked, "Why, there's nothing the matter with this horse; he's a plumb gentle horse." Then Ben fell slightly behind and I heard Sylvane again, "That's all right! Come along! Here, you! Go on, you! Hi, hi, fellows, help me out! he's lying on me!" Sure enough, he was; and when we dragged Sylvane from under him the first thing the rescued Sylvane did was to execute a war-dance, spurs and all, on the iniquitous Ben. We could do nothing with him that day; subsequently we got him so that we could ride him; but he never became a nice saddle-horse.

As with all other forms of work, so on the round-up, a man of ordinary power, who nevertheless does not shirk things merely because they are disagreeable or irksome, soon earns his place. There were crack riders and ropers who, just because they felt such overweening pride in their own prowess, were not really very valuable men. Continually on the circles a cow or a calf would get into some thick patch of bulberry bush and refuse to come out; or when it was getting late we would pass some bad lands that would probably not contain cattle, but might; or a steer would turn fighting mad, or a calf grow tired and want to lie down. If in such a case the man steadily persists in doing the unattractive thing, and after two hours of exasperation and harassment does finally get the cow out, and keep her out, of the bulberry bushes, and drives her to the wagon, or finds some animals that have been passed by in the fourth or fifth patch of bad lands he hunts through, or gets the calf up on his saddle and takes it in anyhow, the foreman soon grows to treat him as having his uses and as being an asset of worth in the round-up, even though neither a fancy roper nor a fancy rider.

When at the Progressive Convention last August, I met George Meyer for the first time in many years, and he recalled to me an incident on one round-up where we happened to be thrown together while driving some cows and calves to camp. When the camp was only just across the river, two of the calves positively refused to go any further. He took one of them in his arms, and after some hazardous manuvering managed to get on his horse, in spite of the objections of the latter, and rode into the river. My calf was too big for such treatment, so in despair I roped it, intending to drag it over. However, as soon as I roped it, the calf started bouncing and bleating, and, owing to some lack of dexterity on my part, suddenly swung round the rear of the horse, bringing the rope under his tail. Down went the tail tight, and the horse "went into figures," as the cow-puncher phrase of that day was. There was a cut bank about four feet high on the hither side of the river, and over this the horse bucked. We went into the water with a splash. With a "pluck" the calf followed, described a parabola in the air, and landed beside us. Fortunately, this took the rope out from under the horse's tail, but left him thoroughly frightened. He could not do much bucking in the stream, for there were one or two places where we had to swim, and the shallows were either sandy or muddy; but across we went, at speed, and the calf made a wake like Pharaoh's army in the Red Sea.

On several occasions we had to fight fire. In the geography books of my youth prairie fires were always portrayed as taking place in long grass, and all living things ran before them. On the Northern cattle plains the grass was never long enough to be a source of danger to man or beast. The fires were nothing like the forest fires in the Northern woods. But they destroyed large quantities of feed, and we had to stop them where possible. The process we usually followed was to kill a steer, split it in two lengthwise, and then have two riders drag each half-steer, the rope of one running from his saddle-horn to the front leg, and that of the other to the hind leg. One of the men would spur this horse over or through the line of fire, and the two would then ride forward, dragging the steer bloody side downward along the line of flame, men following on foot with slickers or wet horse-blankets, to beat out any flickering blaze that was still left. It was exciting work, for the fire and the twitching and plucking of the ox carcass over the uneven ground maddened the fierce little horses so that it was necessary to do some riding in order to keep them to their work. After a while it also became very exhausting, the thirst and fatigue being great, as, with parched lips and blackened from head to foot, we toiled at our task.

In those years the Stockman's Association of Montana was a powerful body. I was the delegate to it from the Little Missouri. The meetings that I attended were held in Miles City, at that time a typical cow town. Stockmen of all kinds attended, including the biggest men in the stock business, men like old Conrad Kohrs, who was and is the finest type of pioneer in all the Rocky Mountain country; and

Granville Stewart, who was afterwards appointed Minister by Cleveland, I think to the Argentine; and "Hashknife" Simpson, a Texan who had brought his cattle, the Hashknife brand, up the trail into our country. He and I grew to be great friends. I can see him now the first time we met, grinning at me as, none too comfortable, I sat a half-broken horse at the edge of a cattle herd we were working. His son Sloan Simpson went to Harvard, was one of the first-class men in my regiment, and afterwards held my commission as Postmaster at Dallas.

At the stockmen's meeting in Miles City, in addition to the big stockmen, there were always hundreds of cowboys galloping up and down the wide dusty streets at every hour of the day and night. It was a picturesque sight during the three days the meetings lasted. There was always at least one big dance at the hotel. There were few dress suits, but there was perfect decorum at the dance, and in the square dances most of the men knew the figures far better than I did. With such a crowd in town, sleeping accommodations of any sort were at a premium, and in the hotel there were two men in every bed. On one occasion I had a roommate whom I never saw, because he always went to bed much later than I did and I always got up much earlier than he did. On the last day, however, he rose at the same time and I saw that he was a man I knew named Carter, and nicknamed "Modesty" Carter. He was a stalwart, good-looking fellow, and I was sorry when later I heard that he had been killed in a shooting row.

When I went West, the last great Indian wars had just come to an end, but there were still sporadic outbreaks here and there, and occasionally bands of marauding young braves were a menace to outlying and lonely settlements. Many of the white men were themselves lawless and brutal, and prone to commit outrages on the Indians. Unfortunately, each race tended to hold all the members of the other race responsible for the misdeeds of a few, so that the crime of the miscreant, red or white, who committed the original outrage too often invited retaliation upon entirely innocent people, and this action would in its turn arouse bitter feeling which found vent in still more indiscriminate retaliation. The first year I was on the Little Missouri some Sioux bucks ran off all the horses of a buffalo-hunter's outfit. One of the buffalo-hunters tried to get even by stealing the horses of a Cheyenne hunting party, and when pursued made for a cow camp, with, as a result, a long-range skirmish between the cowboys and the Cheyennes. One of the latter was wounded; but this particular wounded man seemed to have more sense than the other participants in the chain of wrong-doing, and discriminated among the whites. He came into our camp and had his wound dressed.

A year later I was at a desolate little mud road ranch on the Deadwood trail. It was kept by a very capable and very forceful woman, with sound ideas of justice and abundantly well able to hold her own. Her husband was a worthless devil, who finally got drunk on some whisky he obtained from an outfit of Missouri bull-whackers—that is, freighters, driving ox wagons. Under the stimulus of the whisky he picked a quarrel with his wife and attempted to beat her. She knocked him down with a stove-lid lifter, and the admiring bull whackers bore him off, leaving the lady in full possession of the ranch. When I visited her she had a man named Crow Joe working for her, a slab-sided, shifty-eyed person who later, as I heard my foreman explain, "skipped the country with a bunch of horses." The mistress of the ranch made first-class buckskin shirts of great durability. The one she made for me, and which I used for years, was used by one of my sons in Arizona a couple of winters ago. I had ridden down into the country after some lost horses, and visited the ranch to get her to make me the buckskin shirt in question. There were, at the moment, three Indians there, Sioux, well behaved and self-respecting, and she explained to me that they had been resting there waiting for dinner, and that a white man had come along and tried to run off their horses. The Indians were on the lookout, however, and, running out, they caught the man; but, after retaking their horses and depriving him of his gun, they let him go. "I don't see why they let him go," exclaimed my hostess. "I don't believe in stealing Indians' horses any more than white folks'; so I told 'em they could go along and hang him—I'd never cheep. Anyhow, I won't charge them anything for their dinner," concluded my hostess. She was in advance of the usual morality of the time and place, which drew a sharp line between stealing citizens' horses and stealing horses from the Government or the Indians.

A fairly decent citizen, Jap Hunt, who long ago met a violent death, exemplified this attitude towards Indians in some remarks I once heard him make. He had started a horse ranch, and had quite honestly purchased a number of broken-down horses of different brands, with the view of doctoring them and selling them again. About this time there had been much horse-stealing and cattle-killing in our Territory and in Montana, and under the direction of some of the big cattle-growers a committee of vigilantes had been organized to take action against the rustlers, as the horse thieves and cattle thieves were called. The vigilantes, or stranglers, as they were locally known, did their work thoroughly; but, as always happens with bodies of the kind, toward the end they grew reckless in their actions, paid off private grudges, and hung men on slight provocation. Riding into Jap Hunt's ranch, they nearly hung him because he had so many horses of different brands. He was finally let off. He was much upset by the incident, and explained again and again, "The idea of saying that I was a horse thief! Why, I never stole a horse in my life-leastways from a white man. I don't count Indians nor the Government, of course." Jap had been reared among men still in the stage of tribal morality, and while they recognized their obligations to one another, both the Government and the Indians seemed alien bodies, in regard to which the laws of morality did not apply.

On the other hand, parties of savage young bucks would treat lonely settlers just as badly, and in addition sometimes murder them. Such a party was generally composed of young fellows burning to distinguish themselves. Some one of their number would have obtained a pass from the Indian Agent allowing him to travel off the reservation, which pass would be flourished whenever their action was questioned by bodies of whites of equal strength. I once had a trifling encounter with such a band. I was making my way along the edge of the bad lands, northward from my lower ranch, and was just crossing a plateau when five Indians rode up over the further rim. The instant they saw me they whipped out their guns and raced full speed at me, yelling and flogging their horses. I was on a favorite horse, Manitou, who was a wise old fellow, with nerves not to be shaken by anything. I at once leaped off him and stood with my rifle ready.

It was possible that the Indians were merely making a bluff and intended no mischief. But I did not like their actions, and I thought it likely that if I allowed them to get hold of me they would at least take my horse and rifle, and possibly kill me. So I waited until they were a hundred yards off and then drew a bead on the first. Indians—and, for the matter of that, white men—do not like to ride in on a man who is cool and means shooting, and in a twinkling every man was lying over the side of his horse, and all five had turned and were galloping backwards, having altered their course as quickly as so many teal ducks.

After this one of them made the peace sign, with his blanket first, and then, as he rode toward me, with his open hand. I halted him at a fair distance and asked him what he wanted. He exclaimed, "How! Me good Injun, me good Injun," and tried to show me the dirty piece of paper on which his agency pass was written. I told him with sincerity that I was glad that he was a good Indian, but that he must not come any closer. He then asked for sugar and tobacco. I told him I had none. Another Indian began slowly drifting toward me in spite of my calling out to keep back, so I once more aimed with my rifle, whereupon both Indians slipped to the other side of their horses and galloped off, with oaths that did credit to at least one side of their acquaintance with

English. I now mounted and pushed over the plateau on to the open prairie. In those days an Indian, although not as good a shot as a white man, was infinitely better at crawling under and taking advantage of cover; and the worst thing a white man could do was to get into cover, whereas out in the open if he kept his head he had a good chance of standing off even half a dozen assailants. The Indians accompanied me for a couple of miles. Then I reached the open prairie, and resumed my northward ride, not being further molested.

In the old days in the ranch country we depended upon game for fresh meat. Nobody liked to kill a beef, and although now and then a maverick yearling might be killed on the round-up, most of us looked askance at the deed, because if the practice of beef-killing was ever allowed to start, the rustlers—the horse thieves and cattle thieves— would be sure to seize on it as an excuse for general slaughter. Getting meat for the ranch usually devolved upon me. I almost always carried a rifle when I rode, either in a scabbard under my thigh, or across the pommel. Often I would pick up a deer or antelope while about my regular work, when visiting a line camp or riding after the cattle. At other times I would make a day's trip after them. In the fall we sometimes took a wagon and made a week's hunt, returning with eight or ten deer carcasses, and perhaps an elk or a mountain sheep as well. I never became more than a fair hunter, and at times I had most exasperating experiences, either failing to see game which I ought to have seen, or committing some blunder in the stalk, or failing to kill when I fired. Looking back, I am inclined to say that if I had any good quality as a hunter it was that of perseverance. "It is dogged that does it" in hunting as in many other things. Unless in wholly exceptional cases, when we were very hungry, I never killed anything but bucks.

Occasionally I made long trips away from the ranch and among the Rocky Mountains with my ranch foreman Merrifield; or in later years with Tazewell Woody, John Willis, or John Goff. We hunted bears, both the black and the grizzly, cougars and wolves, and moose, wapiti, and white goat. On one of these trips I killed a bison bull, and I also killed a bison bull on the Little Missouri some fifty miles south of my ranch on a trip which Joe Ferris and I took together. It was rather a rough trip. Each of us carried only his slicker behind him on the saddle, with some flour and bacon done up in it. We met with all kinds of misadventures. Finally one night, when we were sleeping by a slimy little prairie pool where there was not a stick of wood, we had to tie the horses to the horns of our saddles; and then we went to sleep with our heads on the saddles. In the middle of the night something stampeded the horses, and away they went, with the saddles after them. As we jumped to our feet Joe eyed me with an evident suspicion that I was the Jonah of the party, and said: "O I've never done anything to deserve this. Did you ever do anything to deserve this?"

In addition to my private duties, I sometimes served as deputy sheriff for the northern end of our county. The sheriff and I crisscrossed in our public and private relations. He often worked for me as a hired hand at the same time that I was his deputy. His name, or at least the name he went by, was Bill Jones, and as there were in the neighborhood several Bill Joneses—Three Seven Bill Jones, Texas Bill Jones, and the like—the sheriff was known as Hell Roaring Bill Jones. He was a thorough frontiersman, excellent in all kinds of emergencies, and a very game man. I became much attached to him. He was a thoroughly good citizen when sober, but he was a little wild when drunk. Unfortunately, toward the end of his life he got to drinking very heavily. When, in 1905, John Burroughs and I visited the Yellowstone Park, poor Bill Jones, very much down in the world, was driving a team in Gardiner outside the park. I had looked forward to seeing him, and he was equally anxious to see me. He kept telling his cronies of our intimacy and of what we were going to do together, and then got drinking; and the result was that by the time I reached Gardiner he had to be carried out and left in the sage-brush. When I came out of the park, I sent on in advance to tell them to be sure to keep him sober, and they did so. But it was a rather sad interview. The old fellow had gone to pieces, and soon after I left he got lost in a blizzard and was dead when they found him.

Bill Jones was a gun-fighter and also a good man with his fists. On one occasion there was an election in town. There had been many threats that the party of disorder would import section hands from the neighboring railway stations to down our side. I did not reach Medora, the forlorn little cattle town which was our county seat, until the election was well under way. I then asked one of my friends if there had been any disorder. Bill Jones was standing by. "Disorder ___!" said my friend. "Bill Jones just stood there with one hand on his gun and the other pointing over toward the new jail whenever any man who didn't have a right to vote came near the polls. There was only one of them tried to vote, and Bill knocked him down. ____!" Added my friend, meditatively, "The way that man fell!" "Well," struck in Bill Jones, "if he hadn't fell I'd have walked round behind him to see what was propping him up!"

In the days when I lived on the ranch I usually spent most of the winter in the East, and when I returned in the early spring I was always interested in finding out what had happened since my departure. On one occasion I was met by Bill Jones and Sylvane Ferris, and in the course of our conversation they mentioned "the lunatic." This led to a question on my part, and Sylvane Ferris began the story: "Well, you see, he was on a train and he shot the newsboy. At first they weren't going to do anything to him, for they thought he just had it in for the newsboy. But then somebody said, 'Why, he's plumb crazy, and he's liable to shoot any of us!' and then they threw him off the train. It was here at Medora, and they asked if anybody would take care of him, and Bill Jones said he would, because he was the sheriff and the jail had two rooms, and he was living in one and would put the lunatic in the other." Here Bill Jones interrupted: "Yes, and more fool me! I wouldn't take charge of another lunatic if the whole county asked me. Why" (with the air of a man announcing an astounding discovery), "that lunatic didn't have his right senses! He wouldn't eat, till me and Snyder got him down on the shavings and made him eat." Snyder was a huge, happy-go-lucky, kind-hearted Pennsylvania Dutchman, and was Bill Jones's chief deputy.

Bill continued: "You know, Snyder's soft-hearted, he is. Well, he'd think that lunatic looked peaked, and he'd take him out for an airing. Then the boys would get joshing him as to how much start he could give him over the prairie and catch him again." Apparently the amount of the start given the lunatic depended upon the amount of the bet to which the joshing led up. I asked Bill what he would have done if Snyder hadn't caught the lunatic. This was evidently a new idea, and he responded that Snyder always did catch him. "Well, but suppose he hadn't caught him?" "Well," said Bill Jones, "if Snyder hadn't caught the lunatic, I'd have whaled _____ out of Snyder!"

Under these circumstances Snyder ran his best and always did catch the patient. It must not be gathered from this that the lunatic was badly treated. He was well treated. He become greatly attached to both Bill Jones and Snyder, and he objected strongly when, after the frontier theory of treatment of the insane had received a full trial, he was finally sent off to the territorial capital. It was merely that all the relations of life in that place and day were so managed as to give ample opportunity for the expression of individuality, whether in sheriff or ranchman. The local practical joker once attempted to have some fun at the expense of the lunatic, and Bill Jones described the result. "You know Bixby, don't you? Well," with deep disapproval, "Bixby thinks he is funny, he does. He'd come and he'd wake that lunatic up at night, and I'd have to get up and soothe him. I fixed Bixby all right, though. I fastened a rope on the latch, and next time Bixby came I let the lunatic out on him. He 'most bit Bixby's nose off. I learned Bixby!"

Bill Jones had been unconventional in other relations besides that of sheriff. He once casually mentioned to me that he had served on the police force of Bismarck, but he had left because he "beat the Mayor over the head with his gun one day." He added: "The Mayor, he didn't mind it, but the Superintendent of Police said he guessed I'd better resign." His feeling, obviously, was that the Superintendent of Police was a martinet, unfit to take large views of life.

It was while with Bill Jones that I first made acquaintance with Seth Bullock. Seth was at that time sheriff in the Black Hills district, and a man he had wanted-a horse thief-I finally got, I being at the time deputy sheriff two or three hundred miles to the north. The man went by a nickname which I will call "Crazy Steve;" a year or two afterwards I received a letter asking about him from his uncle, a thoroughly respectable man in a Western State; and later this uncle and I met at Washington when I was President and he a United States Senator. It was some time after "Steve's" capture that I went down to Deadwood on business, Sylvane Ferris and I on horseback, while Bill Jones drove the wagon. At a little town, Spearfish, I think, after crossing the last eighty or ninety miles of gumbo prairie, we met Seth Bullock. We had had rather a rough trip, and had lain out for a fortnight, so I suppose we looked somewhat unkempt. Seth received us with rather distant courtesy at first, but unbent when he found out who we were, remarking, "You see, by your looks I thought you were some kind of a tin-horn gambling outfit, and that I might have to keep an eye on you!" He then inquired after the capture of "Steve"—with a little of the air of one sportsman when another has shot a quail that either might have claimed—"My bird, I believe?" Later Seth Bullock became, and has ever since remained, one of my stanchest and most valued friends. He served as Marshal for South Dakota under me as President. When, after the close of my term, I went to Africa, on getting back to Europe I cabled Seth Bullock to bring over Mrs. Bullock and meet me in London, which he did; by that time I felt that I just had to meet my own people, who spoke my neighborhood dialect.

When serving as deputy sheriff I was impressed with the advantage the officer of the law has over ordinary wrong-doers, provided he thoroughly knows his own mind. There are exceptional outlaws, men with a price on their heads and of remarkable prowess, who are utterly indifferent to taking life, and whose warfare against society is as open as that of a savage on the war-path. The law officer has no advantage whatever over these men save what his own prowess may— or may not—give him. Such a man was Billy the Kid, the notorious man-killer and desperado of New Mexico, who was himself finally slain by a friend of mine, Pat Garrett, whom, when I was President, I made collector of customs at El Paso. But the ordinary criminal, even when murderously inclined, feels just a moment's hesitation as to whether he cares to kill an officer of the law engaged in his duty. I took in more than one man who was probably a better man than I was with both rifle and revolver; but in each case I knew just what I wanted to do, and, like David Harum, I "did it first," whereas the fraction of a second that the other man hesitated put him in a position where it was useless for him to resist.

I owe more than I can ever express to the West, which

of course means to the men and women I met in the West. There were a few people of bad type in my neighborhood-that would be true of every group of men, even in a theological seminary—but I could not speak with too great affection and respect of the great majority of my friends, the hard-working men and women who dwelt for a space of perhaps a hundred and fifty miles along the Little Missouri. I was always as welcome at their houses as they were at mine. Everybody worked, everybody was willing to help everybody else, and yet nobody asked any favors. The same thing was true of the people whom I got to know fifty miles east and fifty miles west of my own range, and of the men I met on the round-ups. They soon accepted me as a friend and fellow-worker who stood on an equal footing with them, and I believe the most of them have kept their feeling for me ever since. No guests were ever more welcome at the White House than these old friends of the cattle ranches and the cow camps—the men with whom I had ridden the long circle and eaten at the tail-board of a chuck-wagon—whenever they turned up at Washington during my Presidency. I remember one of them who appeared at Washington one day just before lunch, a huge, powerful man who, when I knew him, had been distinctly a fighting character. It happened that on that day another old friend, the British Ambassador, Mr. Bryce, was among those coming to lunch. Just before we went in I turned to my cow-puncher friend and said to him with great solemnity, "Remember, Jim, that if you shot at the feet of the British Ambassador to make him dance, it would be likely to cause international complications;" to which Jim responded with unaffected horror, "Why, Colonel, I shouldn't think of it, I shouldn't think of it!"

Not only did the men and women whom I met in the cow country quite unconsciously help me, by the insight which working and living with them enabled me to get into the mind and soul of the average American of the right type, but they helped me in another way. I made up my mind that the men were of just the kind whom it would be well to have with me if ever it became necessary to go to war. When the Spanish War came, I gave this thought practical realization.

Fortunately, Wister and Remington, with pen and pencil, have made these men live as long as our literature lives. I have sometimes been asked if Wister's "Virginian" is not overdrawn; why, one of the men I have mentioned in this chapter was in all essentials the Virginian in real life, not only in his force but in his charm. Half of the men I worked with or played with and half of the men who soldiered with me afterwards in my regiment might have walked out of Wister's stories or Remington's pictures.

There were bad characters in the Western country at that time, of course, and under the conditions of life they were probably more dangerous than they would have been elsewhere. I hardly ever had any difficulty, however. I never went into a saloon, and in the little hotels I kept out of the bar-room unless, as sometimes happened, the bar-room was the only room on the lower floor except the dining-room. I always endeavored to keep out of a quarrel until self-respect forbade my making any further effort to avoid it, and I very rarely had even the semblance of trouble.

Of course amusing incidents occurred now and then.

Usually these took place when I was hunting lost horses, for in hunting lost horses I was ordinarily alone, and occasionally had to travel a hundred or a hundred and fifty miles away from my own country. On one such occasion I reached a little cow town long after dark, stabled my horse in an empty outbuilding, and when I reached the hotel was informed in response to my request for a bed that I could have the last one left, as there was only one other man in it. The room to which I was shown contained two double beds; one contained two men fast asleep, and the other only one man, also asleep. This man proved to be a friend, one of the Bill Joneses whom I have previously mentioned. I undressed according to the fashion of the day and place, that is, I put my trousers, boots, shaps, and gun down beside the bed, and turned in. A couple of hours later I was awakened by the door being thrown open and a lantern flashed in my face, the light gleaming on the muzzle of a cocked .45. Another man said to the lantern-bearer, "It ain't him;" the next moment my bedfellow was covered with two guns, and addressed, "Now, Bill, don't make a fuss, but come along quiet." "I'm not thinking of making a fuss," said Bill. "That's right," was the answer; "we're your friends; we don't want to hurt you; we just want you to come along, you know why." And Bill pulled on his trousers and boots and walked out with them. Up to this time there had not been a sound from the other bed. Now a match was scratched, a candle lit, and one of the men in the other bed looked round the room. At this point I committed the breach of etiquette of asking questions. "I wonder why they took Bill," I said. There was no answer, and I repeated, "I wonder why they took Bill." "Well," said the man with the candle, dryly, "I reckon they wanted him," and with that he blew out the candle and conversation ceased. Later I discovered that Bill in a fit of playfulness had held up the Northern Pacific train at a near-by station by shooting at the feet of the conductor to make him dance. This was purely a joke on Bill's part, but the Northern Pacific people possessed a less robust sense of humor, and on their complaint the United States Marshal was sent after Bill, on the ground that by delaying the train he had interfered with the mails.

The only time I ever had serious trouble was at an even more primitive little hotel than the one in question. It was also on an occasion when I was out after lost horses. Below the hotel had merely a bar-room, a dining-room, and a lean-to kitchen; above was a loft with fifteen or twenty beds in it. It was late in the evening when I reached the place. I heard one or two shots in the bar-room as I came up, and I disliked going in. But there was nowhere else to go, and it was a cold night. Inside the room were several men, who, including the bartender, were wearing the kind of smile worn by men who are making believe to like what they don't like. A shabby individual in a broad hat with a cocked gun in each hand was walking up and down the floor talking with strident profanity. He had evidently been shooting at the clock, which had two or three holes in its face.

He was not a "bad man" of the really dangerous type, the true man-killer type, but he was an objectionable creature, a would-be bad man, a bully who for the moment was having things all his own way. As soon as he saw me he hailed me as "Four eyes," in reference to my spectacles, and said, "Four eyes is going to treat." I joined in the laugh and got behind the stove and sat down, thinking to escape notice. He followed me, however, and though I tried to pass it off as a jest this merely made him more offensive, and he stood leaning over me, a gun in each hand, using very foul language. He was foolish to stand so near, and, moreover, his heels were close together, so that his position was unstable. Accordingly, in response to his reiterated command that I should set up the drinks, I said, "Well, if I've got to, I've got to," and rose, looking past him.

As I rose, I struck quick and hard with my right just to one side of the point of his jaw, hitting with my left as I straightened out, and then again with my right. He fired the guns, but I do not know whether this was merely a convulsive action of his hands or whether he was trying to shoot at me. When he went down he struck the corner of the bar with his head. It was not a case in which one could afford to take chances, and if he had moved I was about to drop on his ribs with my knees; but he was senseless. I took away his guns, and the other people in the room, who were now loud in their denunciation of him, hustled him out and put him in a shed. I got dinner as soon as possible, sitting in a corner of the dining-room away from the windows, and then went upstairs to bed where it was dark so that there would be no chance of any one shooting at me from the outside. However, nothing happened. When my assailant came to, he went down to the station and left on a freight.

As I have said, most of the men of my regiment were just such men as those I knew in the ranch country; indeed, some of my ranch friends were in the regiment—Fred Herrig, the forest ranger, for instance, in whose company I

shot my biggest mountain ram. After the regiment was
disbanded the careers of certain of the men were diversified
by odd incidents. Our relations were of the friendliest, and,
as they explained, they felt "as if I was a father" to them.
The manifestations of this feeling were sometimes less
attractive than the phrase sounded, as it was chiefly used by
the few who were behaving like very bad children indeed.
The great majority of the men when the regiment
disbanded took up the business of their lives where they had
dropped it a few months previously, and these men merely
tried to help me or help one another as the occasion arose;
no man ever had more cause to be proud of his regiment
than I had of mine, both in war and in peace. But there was
a minority among them who in certain ways were unsuited
for a life of peaceful regularity, although often enough they
had been first-class soldiers.

It was from these men that letters came with a
stereotyped opening which always caused my heart to
sink—"Dear Colonel: I write you because I am in trouble."
The trouble might take almost any form. One
correspondent continued: "I did not take the horse, but
they say I did." Another complained that his mother-in-law
had put him in jail for bigamy. In the case of another the
incident was more markworthy. I will call him Gritto. He
wrote me a letter beginning: "Dear Colonel: I write you
because I am in trouble. I have shot a lady in the eye. But,
Colonel, I was not shooting at the lady. I was shooting at
my wife," which he apparently regarded as a sufficient
excuse as between men of the world. I answered that I drew
the line at shooting at ladies, and did not hear any more of

the incident for several years.

Then, while I was President, a member of the regiment, Major Llewellyn, who was Federal District Attorney under me in New Mexico, wrote me a letter filled, as his letters usually were, with bits of interesting gossip about the comrades. It ran in part as follows

"Since I last wrote you Comrade Ritchie has killed a man in Colorado. I understand that the comrade was playing a poker game, and the man sat into the game and used such language that Comrade Ritchie had to shoot. Comrade Webb has killed two men in Beaver, Arizona. Comrade Webb is in the Forest Service, and the killing was in the line of professional duty. I was out at the penitentiary the other day and saw Comrade Gritto, who, you may remember, was put there for shooting his sister-in-law [this was the first information I had had as to the identity of the lady who was shot in the eye]. Since he was in there Comrade Boyne has run off to old Mexico with his (Gritto's) wife, and the people of Grant County think he ought to be let out." Evidently the sporting instincts of the people of Grant County had been roused, and they felt that, as Comrade Boyne had had a fair start, the other comrade should be let out in order to see what would happen.

The men of the regiment always enthusiastically helped me when I was running for office. On one occasion Buck Taylor, of Texas, accompanied me on a trip and made a speech for me. The crowd took to his speech from the beginning and so did I, until the peroration, which ran as follows: "My fellow-citizens, vote for my Colonel! vote for my Colonel! and he will lead you, as he led us, like sheep to the slaughter!" This hardly seemed a tribute to my military skill; but it delighted the crowd, and as far as I could tell did me nothing but good.

On another tour, when I was running for Vice-President, a member of the regiment who was along on the train got into a discussion with a Populist editor who had expressed an unfavorable estimate of my character, and in the course of the discussion shot the editor-not fatally. We had to leave him to be tried, and as he had no money I left him $150 to hire counsel-having borrowed the money from Senator Wolcott, of Colorado, who was also with me. After election I received from my friend a letter running: "Dear Colonel: I find I will not have to use that $150 you lent me, as we have elected our candidate for District Attorney. So I have used it to settle a horse transaction in which I unfortunately became involved." A few weeks later, however, I received a heartbroken letter setting forth the fact that the District Attorney—whom he evidently felt to be a cold-blooded formalist—had put him in jail. Then the affair dropped out of sight until two or three years later, when as President I visited a town in another State, and the leaders of the delegation which received me included both my correspondent and the editor, now fast friends, and both of them ardent supporters of mine.

At one of the regimental reunions a man, who had been an excellent soldier, in greeting me mentioned how glad he was that the judge had let him out in time to get to the reunion. I asked what was the matter, and he replied with some surprise: "Why, Colonel, don't you know I had a difficulty with a gentleman, and ... er ... well, I killed the gentleman. But you can see that the judge thought it was all right or he wouldn't have let me go." Waiving the latter point, I said: "How did it happen? How did you do it?" Misinterpreting my question as showing an interest only in the technique of the performance, the ex-puncher replied: "With a .38 on a .45 frame, Colonel." I chuckled over the answer, and it became proverbial with my family and some of my friends, including Seth Bullock. When I was shot at Milwaukee, Seth Bullock wired an inquiry to which I responded that it was all right, that the weapon was merely "a .38 on a .45 frame." The telegram in some way became public, and puzzled outsiders. By the way, both the men of my regiment and the friends I had made in the old days in the West were themselves a little puzzled at the interest shown in my making my speech after being shot. This was what they expected, what they accepted as the right thing for a man to do under the circumstances, a thing the non-performance of which would have been discreditable rather than the performance being creditable. They would not have expected a man to leave a battle, for instance, because of being wounded in such fashion; and they saw no reason why he should abandon a less important and less risky duty.

One of the best soldiers of my regiment was a huge man whom I made marshal of a Rocky Mountain State. He had spent his hot and lusty youth on the frontier during its viking age, and at that time had naturally taken part in incidents which seemed queer to men "accustomed to die decently of zymotic diseases." I told him that an effort would doubtless be made to prevent his confirmation by the

Senate, and therefore that I wanted to know all the facts in his case. Had he played faro? He had; but it was when everybody played faro, and he had never played a brace game. Had he killed anybody? Yes, but it was in Dodge City on occasions when he was deputy marshal or town marshal, at a time when Dodge City, now the most peaceful of communities, was the toughest town on the continent, and crowded with man-killing outlaws and road agents; and he produced telegrams from judges of high character testifying to the need of the actions he had taken. Finally I said: "Now, Ben, how did you lose that half of your ear?" To which, looking rather shy, he responded: "Well, Colonel, it was bit off." "How did it happen, Ben?" "Well, you see, I was sent to arrest a gentleman, and him and me mixed it up, and he bit off my ear." "What did you do to the gentleman, Ben?" And Ben, looking more coy than ever, responded: "Well, Colonel, we broke about even!" I forebore to inquire what variety of mayhem he had committed on the "gentleman." After considerable struggle I got him confirmed by the Senate, and he made one of the best marshals in the entire service, exactly as he had already made one of the best soldiers in the regiment; and I never wish to see a better citizen, nor a man in whom I would more implicitly trust in every way.

When, in 1900, I was nominated for Vice-President, I was sent by the National Committee on a trip into the States of the high plains and the Rocky Mountains. These had all gone overwhelmingly for Mr. Bryan on the free-silver issue four years previously, and it was thought that I, because of my knowledge of and acquaintanceship with the people, might accomplish something towards bringing them back into line. It was an interesting trip, and the monotony usually attendant upon such a campaign of political speaking was diversified in vivid fashion by occasional hostile audiences. One or two of the meetings ended in riots. One meeting was finally broken up by a mob; everybody fought so that the speaking had to stop. Soon after this we reached another town where we were told there might be trouble. Here the local committee included an old and valued friend, a "two-gun" man of repute, who was not in the least quarrelsome, but who always kept his word. We marched round to the local opera-house, which was packed with a mass of men, many of them rather rough-looking. My friend the two-gun man sat immediately behind me, a gun on each hip, his arms folded, looking at the audience; fixing his gaze with instant intentness on any section of the house from which there came so much as a whisper. The audience listened to me with rapt attention. At the end, with a pride in my rhetorical powers which proceeded from a misunderstanding of the situation, I remarked to the chairman: "I held that audience well; there wasn't an interruption." To which the chairman replied: "Interruption? Well, I guess not! Seth had sent round word that if any son of a gun peeped he'd kill him!"

There was one bit of frontier philosophy which I should like to see imitated in more advanced communities. Certain crimes of revolting baseness and cruelty were never forgiven. But in the case of ordinary offenses, the man who had served his term and who then tried to make good was given a fair chance; and of course this was equally true of the women. Every one who has studied the subject at all is only too well aware that the world offsets the readiness with which it condones a crime for which a man escapes punishment, by its unforgiving relentlessness to the often far less guilty man who is punished, and who therefore has made his atonement. On the frontier, if the man honestly tried to behave himself there was generally a disposition to give him fair play and a decent show. Several of the men I knew and whom I particularly liked came in this class. There was one such man in my regiment, a man who had served a term for robbery under arms, and who had atoned for it by many years of fine performance of duty. I put him in a high official position, and no man under me rendered better service to the State, nor was there any man whom, as soldier, as civil officer, as citizen, and as friend, I valued and respected—and now value and respect—more.

Now I suppose some good people will gather from this that I favor men who commit crimes. I certainly do not favor them. I have not a particle of sympathy with the sentimentality—as I deem it, the mawkishness—which overflows with foolish pity for the criminal and cares not at all for the victim of the criminal. I am glad to see wrong-doers punished. The punishment is an absolute necessity from the standpoint of society; and I put the reformation of the criminal second to the welfare of society. But I do desire to see the man or woman who has paid the penalty and who wishes to reform given a helping hand-surely every one of us who knows his own heart must know that he too may stumble, and should be anxious to help his brother or sister who has stumbled. When the criminal has been punished, if he then shows a sincere desire to lead a decent and upright life, he should be given the chance, he should be helped and not hindered; and if he makes good, he should receive that respect from others which so often aids in creating self-respect—the most invaluable of all possessions.

PART III:
OBSERVATIONS ON BOYHOOD AND CHARACTER

THE STRENUOUS LIFE

In Chicago on April 10, 1899 Roosevelt gave a speech entitled The Strenuous Life. In it he outlined his philosophy of life and his attitude toward US expansionism. Following is part of that speech as published in the New York Times on April 11, 1899—D.W.P.

In speaking to you, men of the greatest city of the West, men of the State which gave to the country Lincoln and Grant, men who pre-eminently and distinctly embody all that is most American in the American character, I wish to preach, not the doctrine of ignoble ease, but the doctrine of the strenuous life, the life of toil and effort, of labor and strife; to preach that highest form of success which comes, not to the man who desires mere easy peace, but to the man who does not shrink from danger, from hardship, or from bitter toil, and who out of these wins the splendid ultimate triumph.

We cannot sit huddled within our borders and avow ourselves merely an assemblage of well-to-do hucksters who care nothing for what happens beyond. Such a policy would defeat even its own end; for as the nations grow to have ever wider and wider interests and are brought into closer and closer contact, if we are to hold our own in the struggle for naval and commercial supremacy, we must build up our power without our own borders. We must build the isthmian canal, and we must grasp the points of vantage which will enable us to have our say in deciding the destiny of the oceans of the East and the West.

If twenty years ago we had gone to war we should have found the navy as absolutely unprepared as the army. But in the early eighties the attention of the Nation became directed to our naval needs. Congress most wisely made a series of appropriations to build up a new navy, and under a succession of able and patriotic Secretaries, of both political parties, the navy was gradually built up, until its material became equal to its splendid personnel, with the result that last Summer it leaped to its proper place as one of the most brilliant and formidable fighting navies in the entire world. Read The Congressional Record. Find out the Senators and Congressmen who opposed the grants for building the new ships, who opposed the purchase of armor, without which the ships were worthless; who opposed any adequate maintenance for the Navy Department, and strove to cut down the number of men necessary to man our fleets. The men who did these things were one and all working to bring disaster on the country. Their motives may or may not have been good, but their acts were heavily fraught with evil. They did ill for the National honor, and we won in spite of their sinister opposition.

Our army has never been built up as it should be built up. I shall not discuss with an audience like this the puerile suggestion that a Nation of seventy millions of freemen is in danger of losing its liberties from the existence of an army of 100,000 men, three-fourths of whom will be employed in certain foreign islands, in certain coast fortresses, and on Indian reservations. No man of good sense and stout heart can take such a proposition seriously. If we are such weaklings as the proposition implies, then we are unworthy of freedom in any event. To no body of men in the United States is the country so much indebted as to the splendid officers and enlisted men of the regular army and navy: there is no body from which the country has less to fear, and none of which it should be prouder, none which it should be more anxious to upbuild.

Our army needs complete reorganization—not merely enlarging—and the reorganization can only come as the result of legislation. A proper general staff should be established, and the positions of ordnance, commissary, and Quartermaster officers should be filled by detail from the line. Above all, the army must be given the chance to exercise in large bodies. Never again should we see, as we saw in the Spanish war, Major Generals in command of divisions who had never before commanded three companies together in the field. If during the years to come any disaster should befall our arms, afloat or ashore, and thereby any shame come to the United States, remember that the blame will lie upon the men whose names appear upon the roll calls of Congress on the wrong side of these great questions.

In the West Indies and the Philippines alike we are confronted by most difficult problems. The problems are different for the different islands. Puerto Rico is not large enough to stand alone. We must govern it wisely and well, primarily in the interest of its own people. Cuba is, in my judgment, entitled ultimately to settle for itself whether it shall be an independent State or an integral portion of the mightiest of republics. But until order and a stable liberty are secured, we must remain in the island to insure them, and infinite tact, judgment, moderation, and courage must be shown by our military and civil representatives in keeping the island pacified, in relentlessly stamping out brigandage, in protecting all alike, and yet in showing proper recognition to the men who fought for Cuban liberty.

The Philippines offer yet a graver problem. Their population includes half-caste and native Christians, warlike Moslems, with wild pagans. I have scant patience with those who fear to undertake the task of governing the Philippines, and who openly avow that they do fear to undertake it, or that they shrink from it, because of the expense and trouble; but I have even scanter patience with those who make a pretense of humanitarianism to hide and cover their timidity, and who cant about 'liberty' and the 'consent of the governed' in order to excuse themselves for their unwillingness to play the part of men. Their doctrines, if carried out, would make it incumbent upon us to leave the Apaches of Arizona to work out their own salvation and to decline to interfere in a single Indian reservation. Their doctrines condemn your forefathers and mine for ever having settled in these United States.

Resistance must be stamped out. The first and all-important work to be done is to establish the supremacy of our flag. We must put down armed resistance before we can accomplish anything else, and there should be no parleying, no faltering in dealing with our foe. As for those in our own country who encourage the foe we can afford contemptuously to disregard them; but it must be remembered that their utterances are saved from being treasonable merely from the fact that they are despicable.

When once we have put down armed resistance, when once our rule is acknowledged, then an even more difficult task will begin, for then we must see to it that the islands are administered with absolute honesty and with good judgment. If we let the public service of the islands be turned into the prey of the spoils politician we shall have begun to tread the path which Spain trod to her own destruction. We must send out there only good and able men, chosen for their fitness and not because of their partisan service, and these men must not only administer impartial justice to the natives and serve their own Government with honesty and fidelity, but most show, the utmost tact and firmness, remembering that with such people as those with whom we are to deal weakness is the greatest of crimes, and that next to weakness comes lack of consideration for their principles and prejudices.

The twentieth century looms before us big with the fate of many nations. Let us therefore boldly face the life of strife, resolute to do our duty well and manfully; resolute to uphold righteousness by deed and by word, resolute to be both honest and brave, to serve high ideals, yet to use practical methods. Above all, let us shrink from no strife, moral or physical, within or without the Nation, provided we are certain that the strife is justified; for it is only through strife, through hard and dangerous endeavor, that we shall ultimately win the goal of true national greatness.

The American Boy

First published in May of 1900, "The American Boy" is an essay in which Teddy extols the virtues of boyhood, and makes an impassioned plea that boys would be trained to live a life of rugged manhood. In a manner reminiscent of G.A. Henty, Roosevelt spoke directly to boys in the most practical and plain manner offering timeless wisdom.—D.W.P.

Of course what we have a right to expect of the American boy is that he shall turn out to be a good American man. Now, the chances are strong that he won't be much of a man unless he is a good deal of a boy. He must not be a coward or a weakling, a bully, a shirk, or a prig. He must work hard and play hard. He must be clean-minded and clean-lived, and able to hold his own under all circumstances and against all comers. It is only on these conditions that he will grow into the kind of American man of whom America can be really proud.

There are always in life countless tendencies for good and for evil, and each succeeding generation sees some of these tendencies strengthened and some weakened; nor is it by any means always, alas! that the tendencies for evil are weakened and those for good strengthened. But during the last few decades there certainly have been some notable changes for good in boy life. The great growth in the love of athletic sports, for instance, while fraught with danger if it becomes one-sided and unhealthy, has beyond all question had an excellent effect in increased manliness. Forty or fifty years ago the writer on American morals was sure to deplore the effeminacy and luxury of young Americans who were born of rich parents. The boy who was well off then, especially in the big Eastern cities, lived too luxuriously, took to billiards as his chief innocent recreation, and felt small shame in his inability to take part in rough pastimes and field-sports. Nowadays, whatever other faults the son of rich parents may tend to develop, he is at least forced by the opinion of all his associates of his own age to bear himself well in manly exercises and to develop his body—and therefore, to a certain extent, his character—in the rough sports which call for pluck, endurance, and physical address.

A boy needs both physical and moral courage. Neither can take the place of the other. When boys become men they will find out that there are some soldiers very brave in the field who have proved timid and worthless as politicians, and some politicians who show an entire readiness to take chances and assume responsibilities in civil affairs, but who lack the fighting edge when opposed to physical danger. In each case, with soldiers and politicians alike, there is but half a virtue. The possession of the courage of the soldier does not excuse the lack of courage in the statesman and, even less does the possession of the courage of the statesman excuse shrinking on the field of battle. Now, this is all just as true of boys. A coward who will take a blow without returning it is a contemptible creature; but, after all, he is hardly as contemptible as the boy who dares not stand up for what he deems right against the sneers of his companions who are themselves wrong. Ridicule is one of the favorite weapons of wickedness, and it is sometimes incomprehensible how good and brave boys will be influenced for evil by the jeers of associates who have no one quality that calls for respect, but who affect to laugh at the very traits which ought to be peculiarly the cause for pride.

There is no need to be a prig. There is no need for a boy to preach about his own good conduct and virtue. If he does he will make himself offensive and ridiculous. But there is urgent need that he should practice decency; that he should be clean and straight, honest and truthful, gentle and tender, as well as brave. If he can once get to a proper understanding of things, he will have a far more hearty contempt for the boy who has begun a course of feeble dissipation, or who is untruthful, or mean, or dishonest, or cruel, than this boy and his fellows can possibly, in return, feel for him. The very fact that the boy should be manly and able to hold his own, that he should be ashamed to submit to bullying without instant retaliation, should, in return, make him abhor any form of bullying, cruelty, or brutality.

There are two delightful books, Thomas Hughes's "Tom Brown at Rugby," and Aldrich's "Story of a Bad Boy," which I hope every boy still reads; and I think American boys will always feel more in sympathy with Aldrich's story, because there is in it none of the fagging, and the bullying which goes with fagging, the account of which, and the acceptance of which, always puzzle an American admirer of Tom Brown.

There is the same contrast between two stories of Kipling's. One, called "Captains Courageous," describes in the liveliest way just what a boy should be and do. The hero is painted in the beginning as the spoiled, over-indulged child of wealthy parents, of a type which we do sometimes unfortunately see, and than which there exist few things more objectionable on the face of the broad earth. This boy is afterward thrown on his own resources, amid wholesome surroundings, and is forced to work hard among boys and men who are real boys and real men doing real work. The effect is invaluable. On the other hand, if one wishes to find types of boys to be avoided with utter dislike, one will find them in another story by Kipling, called "Stalky & Co.," a story which ought never to have been written, for there is hardly a single form of meanness which it does not seem to extol, or of school mismanagement which it does not seem to applaud. Bullies do not make brave men; and boys or men of foul life cannot become good citizens, good Americans, until they change; and even after the change scars will be left on their souls

The boy can best become a good man by being a good boy—not a goody-goody boy, but just a plain good boy. I do not mean that he must love only the negative virtues; I mean he must love the positive virtues also. "Good," in the largest   sense,   should   include   whatever   is   fine, straightforward, clean, brave, and manly. The best boys I know—the best men I know—are good at their studies or their business, fearless and stalwart, hated and feared by all that is wicked and depraved, incapable of submitting to wrong-doing, and equally incapable of being aught but tender to the weak and helpless. A healthy-minded boy should feel hearty contempt for the coward, and even more hearty indignation for the boy who bullies girls or small boys, or tortures animals. One prime reason for abhorring cowards is because every good boy should have it in him to thrash the objectionable boy as the need arises.

Of course the effect that a thoroughly manly, thoroughly straight and upright boy can have upon the companions of his own age, and upon those who are younger, is incalculable. If he is not thoroughly manly, then they will not respect him, and his good qualities will count for but little; while, of course, if he is mean, cruel, or wicked, then his physical strength and force of mind merely make him so much the more objectionable a member of society. He cannot do good work if he is not strong and does not try with his whole heart and soul to count in any contest; and his strength will be a curse to himself and to every one else if he does not have thorough command over himself and over his own evil passions, and if he does not use his strength on the side of decency, justice, and fair dealing.

In short, in life, as in a foot-ball game, the principle to follow is:

Hit the line hard; don't foul and don't shirk, but hit the line hard!

CHARACTER AND SUCCESS

Roosevelt was known as a man who overcame physical infirmity as a boy, and developed into something of a genius as an adult. Nonetheless, consistent with his Christian upbringing, T.R. viewed both strength and mental prowess as relatively insignificant for a man's success in comparison with strength of character.—D.W.P.

A year or two ago I was speaking to a famous Yale professor, one of the most noted scholars in the country, and one who is even more than a scholar, because he is in every sense of the word a man. We had been discussing the Yale-Harvard foot-ball teams, and he remarked of a certain player: "I told them not to take him, for he was slack in his studies, and my experience is that, as a rule, the man who is slack in his studies will be slack in his foot-ball work; it is character that counts in both."

Bodily vigor is good, and vigor of intellect is even better, but far above both is character. It is true, of course, that a genius may, on certain lines, do more than a brave and manly fellow who is not a genius; and so, in sports, vast physical strength may overcome weakness, even though the puny body may have in it the heart of a lion. But, in the long run, in the great battle of life, no brilliancy of intellect, no perfection of bodily development, will count when weighed in the balance against that assemblage of virtues, active and passive, of moral qualities, which we group together under the name of character; and if between any two contestants, even in college sport or in college work, the difference in character on the right side is as great as the difference of intellect or strength the other way, it is the character side that will win.

Of course this does not mean that either intellect or bodily vigor can safely be neglected. On the contrary, it means that both should be developed, and that not the least of the benefits of developing both comes from the indirect effect which this development itself has upon the character. In very rude and ignorant communities all schooling is more or less looked down upon; but there are now very few places indeed in the United States where elementary schooling is not considered a necessity. There are any number of men, however, priding themselves upon being "hard-headed" and "practical," who sneer at book-learning and at every form of higher education, under the impression that the additional mental culture is at best useless, and is ordinarily harmful in practical life. Not long ago two of the wealthiest men in the United States publicly committed themselves to the proposition that to go to college was a positive disadvantage for a young man who strove for success. Now, of course, the very most successful men we have ever had, men like Lincoln, had no chance to go to college, but did have such indomitable tenacity and such keen appreciation of the value of wisdom that they set to work and learned for themselves far more than they could have been taught in any academy. On the other hand, boys of weak fiber, who go to high school or college instead of going to work after getting through the primary schools, may be seriously damaged instead of benefited. But, as a rule, if the boy has in him the right stuff, it is a great advantage to him should his circumstances be so fortunate as to enable him to get the years of additional mental training. The trouble with the two rich men whose views are above quoted was that, owing largely perhaps to their own defects in early training, they did not know what success really was. Their speeches merely betrayed their own limitations, and did not furnish any argument against education. Success must always include, as its first element, earning a competence for the support of the man himself, and for the bringing up of those dependent upon him. In the vast majority of cases it ought to include financially rather more than this. But the acquisition of wealth is not in the least the only test of success. After a certain amount of wealth has been accumulated, the accumulation of more is of very little consequence indeed from the standpoint of success, as success should be understood both by the community and the individual. Wealthy men who use their wealth aright are a great power for good in the community, and help to upbuild that material national prosperity which must underlie national greatness; but if this were the only kind of success, the nation would be indeed poorly off. Successful statesmen, soldiers, sailors, explorers, historians, poets, and scientific men are also essential to national greatness, and, in fact, very much more essential than any mere successful business man can possibly be. The average man, into whom the average boy develops, is, of course, not going to be a marvel in any line, but, if he only chooses to try, he can be very good in any line, and the chances of his doing good work are immensely increased if he has trained his mind. Of course, if, as a result of his high-school, academy, or college experience, he gets to thinking that the only kind of learning is that to be found in books, he will do very little; but if he keeps his mental balance,—that is, if he shows character,—he will understand both what learning can do and what it cannot, and he will be all the better the more he can get.

A good deal the same thing is true of bodily development. Exactly as one kind of man sneers at college work because he does not think it bears any immediate fruit in money-getting, so another type of man sneers at college sports because he does not see their immediate effect for good in practical life. Of course, if they are carried to an excessive degree, they are altogether bad. It is a good thing for a boy to have captained his school or college eleven, but it is a very bad thing if, twenty years afterward, all that can be said of him is that he has continued to take an interest in foot-ball, base-ball, or boxing, and has with him the memory that he was once captain. A very acute observer has pointed out that, not impossibly, excessive devotion to sports and games has proved a serious detriment in the British army, by leading the officers and even the men to neglect the hard, practical work of their profession for the sake of racing, foot-ball, base-ball, polo, and tennis-until they received a very rude awakening at the hands of the

Boers. Of course this means merely that any healthy pursuit can be abused. The student in a college who "crams" in order to stand at the head of his class, and neglects his health and stunts his development by working for high marks, may do himself much damage; but all that he proves is that the abuse of study is wrong. The fact remains that the study itself is essential. So it is with vigorous pastimes. If rowing or foot-ball or base-ball is treated as the end of life by any considerable section of a community, then that community shows itself to be in an unhealthy condition. If treated as it should be,—that is, as good, healthy play,—it is of great benefit, not only to the body, but in its effect upon character. To study hard implies character in the student, and to work hard at a sport which entails severe physical exertion and steady training also implies character.

All kinds of qualities go to make up character, for, emphatically, the term should include the positive no less than the negative virtues. If we say of a boy or a man, "He is of good character," we mean that he does not do a great many things that are wrong, and we also mean that he does do a great many things which imply much effort of will and readiness to face what is disagreeable. He must not steal, he must not be intemperate, he must not be vicious in any way; he must not be mean or brutal; he must not bully the weak. In fact, he must refrain from whatever is evil. But besides refraining from evil, he must do good. He must be brave and energetic; he must be resolute and persevering. The Bible always inculcates the need of the positive no less than the negative virtues, although certain people who profess to teach Christianity are apt to dwell wholly on the negative.

We are bidden not merely to be harmless as doves, but also as wise as serpents. It is very much easier to carry out the former part of the order than the latter; while, on the other hand, it is of much more importance for the good of mankind that our goodness should be accompanied by wisdom than that we should merely be harmless. If with the serpent wisdom we unite the serpent guile, terrible will be the damage we do; and if, with the best of intentions, we can only manage to deserve the epithet of "harmless," it is hardly worth while to have lived in the world at all.

Perhaps there is no more important component of character than steadfast resolution. The boy who is going to make a great man, or is going to count in any way in after life, must make up his mind not merely to overcome a thousand obstacles, but to win in spite of a thousand repulses or defeats. He may be able to wrest success along the lines on which he originally started. He may have to try something entirely new. On the one hand, he must not be volatile and irresolute, and, on the other hand, he must not fear to try a new line because he has failed in another. Grant did well as a boy and well as a young man; then came a period of trouble and failure, and then the Civil War and his opportunity; and he grasped it, and rose until his name is among the greatest in our history. Young Lincoln, struggling against incalculable odds, worked his way up, trying one thing and another until he, too, struck out boldly into the turbulent torrent of our national life, at a time when only the boldest and wisest could so carry themselves as to win success and honor; and from the struggle he won both death and honor, and stands forevermore among the greatest of mankind.

Character is shown in peace no less than in war. As the greatest fertility of invention, the greatest perfection of armament, will not make soldiers out of cowards, so no mental training and no bodily vigor will make a nation great if it lacks the fundamental principles of honesty and moral cleanliness. After the death of Alexander the Great nearly all of the then civilized world was divided among the Greek monarchies ruled by his companions and their successors. This Greek world was very brilliant and very wealthy. It contained haughty military empires, and huge trading cities, under republican government, which attained the highest pitch of commercial and industrial prosperity. Art flourished to an extraordinary degree; science advanced as never before. There were academies for men of letters; there were many orators, many philosophers. Merchants and business men throve apace, and for a long period the Greek soldiers kept the superiority and renown they had won under the mighty conqueror of the East. But the heart of the people was incurably false, incurably treacherous and debased. Almost every statesman had his price, almost every soldier was a mercenary who, for a sufficient inducement, would betray any cause. Moral corruption ate into the whole social and domestic fabric, until, a little more than a century after the death of Alexander, the empire which he had left had become a mere glittering shell, which went down like a house of cards on impact with the Romans; for the Romans, with all their faults, were then a thoroughly manly race—a race of strong, virile character.

Alike for the nation and the individual, the one indispensable requisite is character—character that does and dares as well as endures, character that is active in the performance of virtue no less than firm in the refusal to do aught that is vicious or degraded.

THE EIGHTH AND NINTH COMMANDMENTS IN POLITICS

Part of Teddy's greatness was his ability to make practical application of biblical principles to public life. In politics, Roosevelt's basic axiom was that absolute honesty on the part of citizens and statesmen alike was the necessary prerequisite for freedom to survive.—D.W.P.

The two commandments which are specially applicable in public life are the eighth and the ninth. Not only every politician, high or low, but every citizen interested in politics, and especially every man who, in a newspaper or on the stump, advocates or condemns any public policy or any public man, should remember always that the two cardinal points in his doctrine ought to be, "Thou shalt not steal," and "Thou shalt not bear false witness against thy neighbor." He should also, of course, remember that the multitude of men who break the moral law expressed in these two commandments are not to be justified because they keep out of the clutches of the human law. Robbery and theft, perjury and subornation of perjury, are crimes punishable by the courts; but many a man who technically never commits any one of these crimes is yet morally quite as guilty as is his less adroit but not more wicked, and possibly infinitely less dangerous, brother who gets into the penitentiary.

As regards the eighth commandment, while the remark of one of the founders of our government, that the whole art of politics consists in being honest, is an overstatement, it remains true that absolute honesty is what Cromwell would have called a "fundamental" of healthy political life. We can afford to differ on the currency, the tariff, and foreign policy; but we cannot afford to differ on the question of honesty if we expect our republic permanently to endure. No community is healthy where it is ever necessary to distinguish one politician among his fellows because "he is honest." Honesty is not so much a credit as an absolute prerequisite to efficient service to the public. Unless a man is honest we have no right to keep him in public life, it matters not how brilliant his capacity, it hardly matters how great his power of doing good service on certain lines may be. Probably very few men will disagree with this statement in the abstract, yet in the concrete there is much wavering about it. The number of public servants who actually take bribes is not very numerous outside of certain well-known centers of festering corruption. But the temptation to be dishonest often comes in insidious ways. There are not a few public men who, though they would repel with indignation an offer of a bribe, will give certain corporations special legislative and executive privileges because they have contributed heavily to campaign funds;

will permit loose and extravagant work because a contractor has political influence; or, at any rate, will permit a public servant to take public money without rendering an adequate return, by conniving at inefficient service on the part of men who are protected by prominent party leaders. Various degrees of moral guilt are involved in the multitudinous actions of this kind; but, after all, directly or indirectly, every such case comes dangerously near the border-line of the commandment which, in forbidding theft, certainly by implication forbids the connivance at theft, or the failure to punish it.

One of the favorite schemes of reformers is to devise some method by which big corporations can be prevented from making heavy subscriptions to campaign funds, and thereby acquiring improper influence. But the best way to prevent them from making contributions for improper purposes is simply to elect as public servants, not professional denouncers of corporations,-for such men are in practice usually their most servile tools,-but men who say, and mean, that they will neither be for nor against corporations; that, on the one hand, they will not be frightened from doing them justice by popular clamor, or, on the other hand, led by any interest whatsoever into doing them more than justice. At the Anti-Trust Conference last summer Mr. Bryan commented, with a sneer, on the fact that "of course" New York would not pass a law prohibiting contributions by corporations. He was right in thinking that New York, while it retains rational civic habits, will not pass ridiculous legislation which cannot be made effective, and which is merely intended to deceive during the campaign the voters least capable of thought. But there will not be the slightest need for such legislation if only the public spirit is sufficiently healthy, sufficiently removed alike from corruption and from demagogy, to see that each corporation receives its exact rights and nothing more; and this is exactly what is now being done in New York by men whom dishonest corporations dread a hundred times more than they dread the demagogic agitators who are a terror merely to honest corporations.

It is, of course, not enough that a public official should be honest. No amount of honesty will avail if he is not also brave and wise. The weakling and the coward cannot be saved by honesty alone; but without honesty the brave and able man is merely a civic wild beast who should be hunted down by every lover of righteousness. No man who is corrupt, no man who condones corruption in others, can possibly do his duty by the community. When this truth is accepted as axiomatic in our politics, then, and not till then, shall we see such a moral uplifting of the people as will render, for instance, Tammany rule in New York, as Tammany rule now is, no more possible than it would be possible to revive the robber baronage of the middle ages.

Great is the danger to our country from the failure among our public men to live up to the eighth commandment, from the callousness in the public which permits such shortcomings. Yet it is not exaggeration to say that the danger is quite as great from those who year in and year out violate the ninth commandment by bearing false witness against the honest man, and who thereby degrade him and elevate the dishonest man until they are both on the same level. The public is quite as much harmed in the one case as in the other, by the one set of wrong-doers as by the other. "Liar" is just as ugly a word as "thief," because it implies the presence of just as ugly a sin in one case as in the other. If a man lies under oath or procures the lie of another under oath, if he perjures himself or suborns perjury, he is guilty under the statute law. Under the higher law, under the great law of morality and righteousness, he is precisely as guilty if, instead of lying in a court, he lies in a newspaper or on the stump; and in all probability the evil effects of his conduct are infinitely more wide-spread and more pernicious. The difference between perjury and mendacity is not in the least one of morals or ethics. It is simply one of legal forms.

The same man may break both commandments, or one group of men may be tempted to break one and another group of men the other. In our civic life the worst offenders against the law of honesty owe no small part of their immunity to those who sin against the law by bearing false witness against their honest neighbors. The sin is, of course, peculiarly revolting when coupled with hypocrisy, when it is committed in the name of morality. Few politicians do as much harm as the newspaper editor, the clergyman, or the lay reformer who, day in and day out, by virulent and untruthful invective aimed at the upholders of honesty, weakens them for the benefit of the frankly vicious. We need fearless criticism of dishonest men, and of honest men on any point where they go wrong; but even more do we need criticism which shall be truthful both in what it says and in what it leaves unsaid—truthful in words and truthful in the impression it designs to leave upon the readers' or hearers' minds.

We need absolute honesty in public life; and we shall not get it until we remember that truth-telling must go hand in hand with it, and that it is quite as important not to tell an untruth about a decent man as it is to tell the truth about one who is not decent.

A MANLY CONFRONTATION

Teddy Roosevelt once shared with his sons that the more challenging aspects of being President was enduring constant criticism and calumnies. Note, however, that Roosevelt not only endured these pressures, but some would say he thrived on them. He possessed that rare gift of leadership which allowed him to transcend negative circumstances, not take criticism personally and to see the best in others. I have included the following commentary by Roosevelt and as an example of the fact that T.R. was not only magnanimous towards his critics, but able to recognize and be grateful for their manly virtues.—D.W.P.

There was a sequel to the "round robin" incident which caused a little stir at the moment; Secretary Alger had asked me to write him freely from time to time. Accordingly, after the surrender of Santiago, I wrote him begging that the cavalry division might be put into the Porto Rican fighting, preparatory to what we supposed would be the big campaign against Havana in the fall. In the letter I extolled the merits of the Rough Riders and of the Regulars, announcing with much complacency that each of our regiments was worth "three of the National Guard regiments, armed with their archaic black powder rifles." 1 Secretary Alger believed, mistakenly, that I had made public the round robin, and was naturally irritated, and I suddenly received from him a published telegram, not alluding to the round robin incident, but quoting my reference to the comparative merits of the cavalry regiments and the National Guard regiments and rebuking me for it. The publication of the extract from my letter was not calculated to help me secure the votes of the National Guard if I ever became a candidate for office. However, I did not mind the matter much, for I had at the time no idea of being a candidate for anything-while in the campaign I ate and drank and thought and dreamed regiment and nothing but regiment, until I got the brigade, and then I devoted all my thoughts to handling the brigade. Anyhow, there was nothing I could do about the matter.

When our transport reached Montauk Point, an army officer came aboard and before doing anything else handed me a sealed letter from the Secretary of War which ran as follows:

War Department,
Washington,
August 10, 1898.

Dear Col. Roosevelt:

You have been a most gallant officer and in the battle before Santiago showed superb soldierly qualities. I would rather add to, than detract from, the honors you have so fairly won, and I wish you all good things. In a moment of aggravation under great stress of feeling, first because I thought you spoke in a disparaging manner of the volunteers (probably without intent, but because of your great enthusiasm for your own men) and second that I believed your published letter would embarrass the Department I sent you a telegram which with an extract from a private letter of yours I gave to the press. I would gladly recall both if I could, but unable to do that I write you this letter which I hope you will receive in the same friendly spirit in which I send it. Come and see me at a very early day. No one will welcome you more heartily than I.

Yours very truly,

(Signed) R. A. Alger

I thought this a manly letter, and paid no more heed to the incident; and when I was President, and General Alger was Senator from Michigan, he was my stanch friend and on most matters my supporter.

Notes